Disney's
FAIRY TALE
Weddings

BY DAVID TUTERA

WITH FASHIONS AND STYLE TIPS BY KIRSTIE KELLY

Disney's

FAIRY TALE

Weddings

by DAVID TUTERA

with FASHIONS and STYLE TIPS by KIRSTIE KELLY

EDITIONS

New York

This book's producers would like to thank Rebekah Belzer, Paulette Cleghorn, Jennifer Eastwood, Liz Hart, Tommi Lewis Tilden, Frankie LoBono, Korri McFann, Jill Rapaport, Netta Scott, and Marybeth Tregarthen.

For information address Disney Editions, 114 Fifth Avenue, New York, New York 10011-5690.
Editorial Director: Wendy Lefkon
Assistant Editor: Jessica Ward

Designed by: Jon Glick, mouse+tiger

Photography by:
Maring Photography — Disney World Dream Wedding, Garden Dream Wedding, Indian Dream Wedding, Sparkle Dream Wedding, Beach Dream Wedding, Modern Dream Wedding, Traditional Dream Wedding, Country Dream Wedding, Asian Dream Wedding, Vintage Hollywood Dream Wedding

Gary Zindel Photography — Sparkle Dream Wedding
Phil Kramer Photographers, Inc. — Sparkle Dream Wedding
Arden Photography — Indian Dream Wedding
Michael Bennett Kress for MBK & Associates — Indian Dream Wedding, Modern Wedding
Geoff Chesman for MBK & Associates — Modern Wedding

Library of Congress Cataloging-in-Publication Data on file

ISBN 978-1-4231-1706-3

First Edition
10 9 8 7 6 5 4 3 2 1
Printed in the United States of America
G942-9090-6-09335

SUSTAINABLE FORESTRY INITIATIVE
Certified Fiber Sourcing
www.sfiprogram.org
PWC-SFICOC-260
For Text Pages Only

The Official Community for Disney Fans
Disney.com/D23

Table of Contents

Disney's Fairy Tale Weddings

MAGIC.

It's more than just illusion. It's the enchantment that comes with discovering breathtaking surprises. It's the journey of the mind to a world of suspended disbelief, where anything is possible. It's the hope that even the most incredible dreams can come true. Proof that magic exists is all around us; it's in beauty, happiness, fate, spirit, and, of course, in love.

A wedding is the essence of all those special elements combined. There's magic in the laughter of a flower girl. The radiance of a bride. The unforgettable look of the groom as he sees his best friend and life love walk down the aisle, and the way time seems to stop as they float upon air, swirling around the dance floor during their first dance. When it comes down to it, all the planning, thought, and effort that brides put into their special day revolve around achieving those special moments. Why? Perhaps we're inspired by a long history of fabled lands and

majestic castles, of princes and princesses and Cinderella stories. Or maybe it's because once you feel the joy of meeting your one true love, you want to share it with the world. Regardless of the reasons, a bride believes in having a magical wedding. And *that's* what my job is all about!

Forever believe in magic?

I do, and so does Disney! Together with Disney's Fairy Tale Weddings, I am pleased to bring you a compilation of my favorite real-life fairy tales about couples just like you, who successfully captured the magic of love and

brought it to their wedding celebrations. If you have ever dreamed of a grand wedding in a storybook setting like these couples did, you'll see that dreams can be a reality for every bride. Your wedding celebration is a reflection of who you are, and I believe that your wedding should tell your story. I'm about to show you how to bring fantasy to life—all it takes is faith, trust, and a touch of pixie dust!

Disney captured my heart in my childhood. I loved watching the fireworks light up the sky over Cinderella's Castle. I remember visiting with my parents and riding the monorail. Any day at Disney World was better than a normal day. I know firsthand how your heart opens and your eyes widen at the sight of Mickey Mouse. There is simply nothing else in the world like the magic of Disney.

Professionally, I've always been inspired by Disney's first-class entertaining. Nothing is ever forgotten. The attention to detail, the flawless service, and the way Disney enables their guests to experience their dreams are what make all the difference.

My career is based on the very same principles of designing exceptional and imaginative parties that create memories to last a lifetime. Starting "The Couture Wedding Collection by David Tutera for Disney's Fairy Tale Weddings" was *my* dream come true. I am thrilled to pair my own wedding-planning experience with the top-tier quality of Disney, and I'm excited to bring this same entertaining magic into your hands for your own weddings at home.

Every bride deserves to be a princess. My general philosophy on wedding planning is that style, taste, and elegance can be achieved at any price, provided you know the right things to do and how to execute them. My ultimate goal for you—the bride and groom—is for you to become guests at your own wedding.

I've created memorable moments for famous celebrities around the world. With this book, I vow to do the same for you, by including tips on every wedding element from the invitation to the last dance. You'll find useful information on ceremonies and receptions, food and cocktails, fashion and beauty, flowers, fabrics, music, and every detail in between. Every aspect of your wedding—including the planning process—should be

just as magical, exciting, and unforgettable as the moment you fell in love.

In addition, bridal gown designer Kirstie Kelly, of Kirstie Kelly for Disney Fairy Tale Weddings, will show you how to look like a princess on your wedding day, whether that means wearing a ball gown inspired by Cinderella, donning a tiara fit for Sleeping Beauty, or choosing crystal chandelier earrings reminiscent of Belle. Kirstie will also share fashion tips to help you and your bridal party look picture-perfect on your special day.

There is much to learn from the royal treatment you get with Disney as you create a similar experience for your own wedding day. Step into the fairy tales of ten very different couples, each with the desire to have a wedding unlike any other. Their stories tell of extraordinary wedding celebrations, including a once-in-a-lifetime royal wedding at Cinderella Castle; an unforgettable tropical ceremony right on the beach; a romantic outdoor candlelit lakeside ceremony; and even a glamorous vintage Hollywood celebration at the Disneyland Resort. In each chapter, you will learn how to apply the same concepts behind these fanciful weddings to your own special day.

Each of your guests will become a believer as they witness your dreams coming true on your wedding day. I can't wait to help you begin telling your own fairy tale, and to send you on your way to your own happily ever after. Forever believe in magic? I do . . . and so will you!

—David Tutera

CHAPTER ONE

A Disney World Dream Wedding

ONCE UPON A TIME, a little girl named Julie dreamed of being a princess on her wedding day. She envisioned being wed in a majestic castle, where a horse-drawn carriage would convey her to her prince, who would be waiting to marry her in the most beautiful of ceremonies. She could almost see and hear every detail of the spectacular royal ball that would follow: a magnificent feast of all her favorite edible delights; elegant music playing as she danced her first dance in a swirling gown; and a ballroom full of crystals and chandeliers, beautiful fabrics, and delicate roses. In Julie's dream, everyone in attendance would celebrate as they shared the happiest day of her life. And she imagined that all of this would take place in the most magical place on earth.

Little did she know that one day, her dreams would come true.

Julie grew up and fell in love with her own Prince Charming, John. And charming he was. He loved her so much that he decided to whisk her away to a land called Florida, to proclaim their true love in front of family, friends, and an entire Magic Kingdom. At Walt Disney World, Julie and John would be the first couple ever to wed at the legendary Cinderella Castle, in front of the park's 40,000 guests. The wedding was set to take place on the most romantic and magical of days: Valentine's Day.

This wedding was also a dream come true from a wedding planner's perspective. Having the opportunity to make the celebration come alive for this special couple in a place that could not be any more perfect for a magical,

royal celebration was truly delightful. Julie was enraptured by the idea of a real princess wedding, which gave us the ability to turn her childhood fantasy into an elegant and unbelievable reality. Our goal was to create a fabulous wedding that, from start to finish, enchanted every guest and made Julie feel like she had stepped into the actual reverie she had imagined since girlhood. With no better place to start than Walt Disney World, we set out to design an extravagant wedding event for the perfect princess bride.

We wanted to not only design a breathtaking royal wedding for Julie, but also a wedding celebration that was exquisitely tailored to who she and John were. No two weddings are ever alike and should be just as individual as the couple. We spent time with the both of them to discover what they loved, what

kind of couple they were, and what elements of their lives would help tell the story of their love to their guests. From their favorite colors to their favorite foods, to Julie's favorite flowers, we gathered all the details on both their personal styles, and their traditions and family heritages. With all these details in hand, we went to work to turn this dream wedding into more than just an extravagant ceremony and a reception, but into a special personal celebration that fit the bride and groom just as perfectly as the glass slipper fit Cinderella's foot.

We based Julie's wedding colors on her favorite color—a rich, deep orange—and then added other complimentary sunset hues such as peaches, pinks, and yellow tones. By bringing out an array of shades with her orange, the strong initial color turned into an overall, well-blended look of sophistication.

On the Cinderella Castle stage where Julie's ceremony would take place, we created several large flower-burst arrangements in these colors to add something special to her ceremony. Such a large stage required large floral arrangements to match, and as the first scene the guests would encounter, it would also need to set a strong precedent for the look of the overall wedding.

On the day of the wedding, the dream ceremony scene was set. Atop seventy-five dark wooden Chiavari chairs, we placed elegant programs that each included a personalized message to the guests from the bride and groom, printed in a beautiful, formal script. The chairs faced a stage adorned with the decadent floral bursts of oranges, pinks, and accent greens. Julie's bridesmaids stood on the stage steps, prepared to surround her in beautifully sleek, peach taffeta gowns that shimmered in the sunlight. Their bouquets specifically complimented their gowns in a unique way; rather than holding traditional bridesmaids' bouquets, Julie's ladies in waiting

held coordinating flowers designed in the shape of mini-handbags.

As the bride prepared for her ceremony, we presented her with a special bridal bouquet of deep orange roses studded with orange Swarovski crystals, white stephanotis, orange lilies, and white calla lilies with the blooms of peach-spray roses placed inside the center of each lily. With John at the castle awaiting his princess, everything was ready for Julie's grand entrance.

Venue Selection

SECOND TO CHOOSING THE MAN YOU WILL MARRY, choosing where your wedding will be is the most important decision a bride can make. As you consider your options, take your time and think carefully. You have total control over this aspect of your wedding. It will allow you to set the scene and create the ambiance that will surround you and your guests as you wed and then dine, dance, and celebrate your love! Your venue will be the backdrop of your wedding, from the place where you exchange your vows to the setting in which you share your first dance as husband and wife. The "where" is essential to the telling of your wedding story, so to help you narrow down choosing the picture-perfect place, consider the following criteria:

CAPACITY. How many people will you have, and what is your budget? As you make your venue decisions for your day of royal treatment, you'll be faced with many options, but first and foremost, your venue must have the capacity to hold all your guests comfortably, as well as provide all the logistical necessities.

YOUR VISION. When you start to consider venues, think back to your original concept of how you pictured yourself getting married. Are you indoors or outdoors? What is the season and what are your surroundings?

STYLE AND COLOR. The desired style of your wedding can be a key factor in determining what location would be appropriate for you. A fun, casual occasion may befit an outdoor summer or fall wedding in a tent. A formal, black-tie affair might be better suited for a hotel ballroom. A bride with a non-traditional dream could be drawn toward a unique venue, like an old theater or a lighthouse.

Whether you're on a castle step or in a chic city loft, your venue is the setting of your story, no matter how traditional or modern your tale.

Julie rode with her father down the famous Main Street, U.S.A.—one of the longest aisles in history—in a gold and white open carriage drawn by four white Shetland ponies (exactly as she dreamed, she later told us). We embellished the back of her carriage with a garland of flowers that matched those that would be seen throughout their wedding and tied the garland with long trailing orange ribbons. The bride graciously waved to park guests who lined the street as they made their way to watch her ceremony.

When the driver helped her out of the carriage, her dress was revealed: a white satin ball gown, tied at the waist with an orange sash flowing down her back (reiterating the orange theme of the event).

In front of thousands of Magic Kingdom guests, six bridesmaids, six groomsmen, and a fourteen-piece band, Julie and John exchanged their vows. It was easy for onlookers to fall in love with the bride and groom; guests witnessed the lighting of the couple's unity candle, an acoustic guitar performance, and a traditional Thai Water Ceremony (a tribute to the bride's Asian background). Two singers harmonized in a performance of "The Prayer" as Julie and John were connected by a flower chain and their officiant performed a *Rod Nam Sang* ceremony. He soaked the couple's hands in water from a conch shell to wish them good fortune and wrapped their hands together with long grasses to symbolize their newfound unity and loyalty to one another, making their ceremony truly unique.

After the bride and groom sealed their vows with a kiss, they rode off on a carriage ride, leading a recessional down their Main Street "aisle." As the band performed during the couple's high-energy departure, bursts of confetti rained down upon a cheering sea of supporters. Several guest books that had been placed throughout the park were filled cover to cover with attendees' signatures and good wishes.

Upon arriving at their evening dinner reception in the Magic Kingdom, Julie and John were shocked with the next surprise we had for them: in the Rose Garden next to Cinderella Castle, we set up their reception under a clear tent, which allowed guests to gaze upon the castle as the evening passed from sunset to starlight. Julie and John would dine with their guests as if they were at a formal royal feast inside the grand ballroom of Cinderella Castle, but with the luxury of being outside under the stars.

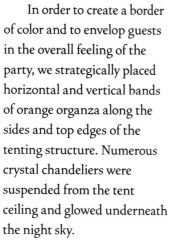

In order to create a border of color and to envelop guests in the overall feeling of the party, we strategically placed horizontal and vertical bands of orange organza along the sides and top edges of the tenting structure. Numerous crystal chandeliers were suspended from the tent ceiling and glowed underneath the night sky.

The regal banquet tables were designed for not just any princess, but specifically for Julie. Julie had told us that she loved gold, so we used that as a predominant touch to make her wedding as lavish as possible.

Tall gold candelabras held large, ornate floral arrangements of dark pink peonies, peach and orange roses, green hydrangea, pink tulips, pink cymbidium orchids, and bursts of pale pink cherry blossoms (reminiscent of the castle-stage ceremony arrangements). Each spherical floral design was framed by four extra tall white taper candles, and strings of dark pink and peach rose petals were suspended from the arrangements along with light pink roping and crystal pendants.

Down the center of each table, correlating singular candlesticks and amber-colored crystal votive candles added more romantic glow, and orchids, roses, and lilies were used to create flower arrangements that stretched the entire length of the tables and onto the floor. Low gold bowls filled with flowers were placed in between the candelabra, which varied the arrangement pattern and enabled guests to see one another. Guests should always notice new things and dimensions of detail on their tables as weddings progress.

The escort card table is a key element that hints to guests what they are about to experience as it is the first impression they get upon arriving at a reception. Therefore,

Clear Tents

ONE OF THE MOST ENCHANTING ways to construct a tent is with a ceiling made out of a clear plastic vinyl that allows the sky and surroundings to show through. Clear tents make the atmosphere seem more open, and they are perfect for outdoor weddings that take place amidst beautiful foliage, skies, or settings. Clear side panels make these tents a very appealing option when you are in a magnificent environment. Light the areas outside the tent and *voila!* You have instant décor. And by using a clear tent, you are also able to spend less on décor because your guests will already be surrounded by beautiful vistas. If you are having a night wedding, add candles or lights to shrubs, trees, and grounds to illuminate your surroundings and bring the outdoors into your area of celebration.

this is a great opportunity to make a "wow" statement. To create a dynamic first experience for Julie and John's guests, we created a decadent double urn arrangement overflowing with flowers amid hundreds of soft rose petals. As each guest entered the tent, a majordomo in a gold tri-cornered hat, fringed jacket, and lace ascot and sleeves announced each guest from a parchment scroll. When the majordomo announced the bride and groom, cocktails commenced. Thirty minutes later, guests took their seats for a royal dining experience.

It was a meal fit for a king. Because long tables create a regal feeling when dining, we brought in four-by-eight-foot rectangular tables that sat eight to ten guests per table. The tables were dressed in custom-designed gold linens in a beautiful antique-style damask fabric trimmed with luxurious gold fringe, and these linens were placed over light pink underlays. Fabric covers that coordinated with the tablecloths adorned the backs of each guest chair.

The place setting was particularly important for this party. Because of the wedding's royal theme and over-the-top extravagance, each piece handled by the guests needed to feel exactly like the dinnerware that a royal family would use. The tables were set with clear glass charger plates featuring dramatic gold embellishments

TUTERA TIP:
Fall is the most amazing time of the year for outdoor weddings laden with natural beauty. A clear tent can enable you to sit underneath canopies of autumn leaves while still dining in a controlled environment. However, do not use a clear tent in hot weather—it can easily become a solarium. Also be aware that clear tents do require several center- and side-support poles, which create more obstructions throughout the tent. For Julie's wedding, we draped the support poles in matching fabric to mask the structure and add more color.

draping used on the tent, and a single rose was placed upon each napkin.

Actualizing the culinary descriptions of the menu cards, Julie and John's chef prepared an elaborate meal for seventy-five, selected especially for the bride and groom. The appetizer of a summer roll with crispy rock shrimp and Nam Pla sauce was a nod to Julie's Thai background—and also one of her favorite dishes. The banana frisée salad playfully and flavorfully depicted a meal Julie and John shared on the night of his proposal. An entrée of braised short rib of beef, signifying one of John's family traditions of preparing this meal on special occasions, delighted the guests while telling them a bit more about the bride and groom in a creative—and quite appetizing way.

reminiscent of the damask pattern on the linen. The white china dinner plates were trimmed in gold and the gold-rimmed crystal-cut stemware matched perfectly. Elegant gilded flatware framed the setting on either side, inviting guests to feel like they were eating among kings and queens.

On top of each setting, a gold damask napkin was arranged into a "pocket fold" in order to display a specialty menu card. The cards featured each guest's name— preceded by "Mademoiselle," "Madame," or "Monsieur"—in beautiful calligraphy, and detailed the courses to come. To polish the look, the cards were folded and tied with orange organza ribbon that matched the fabric

When it came to the last course of Julie and John's dinner, we wanted them to have a cake fit for a king and queen (and eat it, too!). The five-tiered round vanilla wedding cake covered in delicately sculpted, vibrantly colored sugar flowers was so statuesque, it rivaled the turrets of Cinderella Castle.

But the evening would not have been complete without a big surprise for Julie and John, and we

wanted the party to go out with a "bang!"
Right at dusk, a single firework went off. One
by one, more fireworks illuminated the sky
with color and light, enthralling guests as they
watched through their clear tented ceiling.
From the highest turret of the castle, Tinker
Bell took her nightly flight, but this time,
she flew directly over Julie and John's dinner
reception to sprinkle some pixie dust over the
spellbound couple.

Fireworks

DISNEY KNOWS QUITE A BIT about making magic appear out of thin air, from the Wishes fireworks at Magic Kingdom to IllumiNations at Epcot. But creating a dazzling display doesn't have to be that complex when it comes to your own wedding. Even just a spark or two of light in the sky can create an awe-inspiring moment for you and your guests. However, keep in mind that fireworks require lots of logistical planning on the part of the host. Most cities and towns require that you register for a permit far in advance, and each venue will have its own regulations. For Julie and John's party, the fireworks had to be detonated from a special location behind the castle and were required to be at least 300 feet from the tent. Do not try this on your own: hire a professional and follow local safety codes.

The cost of a fireworks display depends on how big of a production you do, as well as the location and the length of the show. Avoid restless guests and keep fireworks to ten minutes or less. If an elaborate sky show isn't in your budget, but you just can't bear to rule out departing in a blaze of glory, know that fireworks don't necessarily have to be the big spectacles that you see at Disney World. Modest displays can be purchased from retailers in many states. Or, if you're looking for low-fuss pyrotechnics, serve sparklers with dessert or have partygoers hold them as you make your grand exit.

Toward the end of the night, the majordomo reappeared to officially proclaim that John and Julie's marriage was the first in history to take place in the Magic Kingdom. He also announced one last surprise: the bride and groom would be the first guests ever to stay in the Cinderella Castle suite. A second fireworks show—complete with heart-shaped pyrotechnics and a farewell from Jiminy Cricket—bid the guests good-night.

When they returned to their rooms, each guest would find a silver and crystal charm of Cinderella's coach resting on their pillow—a favor from Julie and John and a fitting end to their celebration.

One bride's dream had come true. She had married her handsome prince on the steps of a beautiful castle, in a magical place, with no detail spared. All that was left for Julie and John was to begin living happily ever after.

Fashion Tip from Kirstie:

While many brides steer clear of strapless gowns, the truth is, a strapless gown makes almost any décolletage look extra happy. The key to a smashingly successful strapless gown is the fit; substantial boning and corseting will ensure you the ability to move freely without having to nervously tug at your gown during photo-ops and on the dance floor. To test the construction of a gown, simply wave your arms in the air. Should the gown slip lower on your bust, you'll know it's not the right fit for you. Continue "test driving" gowns until you find one that stays put!

OVERVIEW:

FASHION:

The bride wore a Paloma Blanca white satin gathered ball gown with a soft sweetheart neckline, tied at the waist with an orange sash. During the ceremony she wore a white lace bolero over her shoulders, and during the reception she kept warm with a white feather off-the-shoulder wrap, tied with satin ribbon.

The bridesmaids wore floor-length taffeta A-line strapless gowns in shimmering peach, with sweetheart necklines.

INVITATION:

The invitations were regal scrolls created with off-white, textured paper with worn sides. They were printed with formal blue calligraphy, rolled, and secured with a tassel or a matching organza ribbon. The scrolls were sent inside mailing tubes, and for a final touch, each was sealed with a monogrammed wax seal. Special postal stamps featured the bridal couple's monogram on a peach background.

COLOR SWATCHES/
FLORAL GUIDE:

COLORS: sunset hues, with deep orange, dark pink, peach, yellow, gold, and light green

FLOWERS: green viburnum, orange lilies, white calla lilies, peach spray roses, pink cherry blossoms, pink tulips, green and pink cymbidium orchids, green hydrangea, dark pink peonies, peach and orange roses, rose petals

SPECIALTY DRINK: THE SWEET NIGHTINGALE

A Thai ginger-basil specialty drink was served in honor of Julie's Thai heritage, and re-named "The Sweet Nightingale" after the song Cinderella sings while performing her chores. Served in double shot glasses rimmed in colored sugar, the mini-cocktails were served on a gold-rimmed charger plate.

½ oz. ginger-basil syrup*

2 oz. vodka

Splash sparkling water

Lychee and fresh basil for garnish

Add ginger-basil syrup, vodka, sparkling water, and ice to cocktail shaker. Stir and strain into cocktail glass. Tuck the basil leaf into the lychee and skewer with a knotted bamboo cocktail pick for garnish.

* For the ginger-basil syrup add 2 cups water, 2 cups sugar, a pound of coarsely chopped ginger, and a handful of fresh basil leaves to saucepan. Bring to a boil, reduce and let simmer for forty-five minutes. Strain liquid through a cheesecloth. Can be refrigerated in a sealed glass jar for up to two weeks.

MENU:

APPETIZER

Summer rolls

Crispy rock shrimp, beets, cucumber, carrot, and basil tossed in miso chile dressing. Served with Nam Pla sauce

SALAD

Banana frisée salad

Crumbled feta, chunks of banana, hearts of palm, frisée, and cilantro leaves tossed in a grapefruit vinaigrette dressing

ENTRÉE

Braised short rib of beef

Braised short rib of beef with crispy crab wontons and a spicy tomato and coconut salad

DESSERT

Wedding cake

Crispy pavlova with Key lime curd, blueberries, basil, and mint

MUSIC SUGGESTIONS:

FIRST DANCE

"So This Is Love" – from *Cinderella*

"L-O-V-E" – Frank Sinatra

FATHER-DAUGHTER DANCE

"(Everything I Do), I Do It for You"
– Bryan Adams

"Beautiful"
– Wayne Brady and Jim Brickman,
inspired by the movie *Cinderella*

MOTHER-SON DANCE

"A Dream Is a Wish Your Heart
Makes" – from *Cinderella*

"Isn't She Lovely" – Stevie Wonder

FAVOR:

Julie and John gave each guest a silver and crystal charm of Cinderella's coach as a memento of their wedding.

DISNEY TOUCHES: *Cinderella*

❀ Make your invitations or menu cards into scrolls for a regal feel right out of *Cinderella*. Julie and John's printed materials were beautifully scripted by a calligrapher. You can bring this touch of formal elegance to your own invitations, either by hiring a professional calligrapher or by doing "digital calligraphy" on your own computer with the proper font choice.

❀ For your grand entrance into your celebration, have a majordomo announce your arrival. To make your bridal party and guests feel like they're attending Prince Charming's ball, have the majordomo greet and introduce everyone at the door.

❀ It's hard to imagine a fairy-tale wedding taking place without fireworks going off as the prince and princess share their first kiss. Bring some of the sparkle to your wedding celebration with a scaled-down show: ask your waitstaff to place a glowing sparkler in each guest's dessert. Or give sparklers to your guests to wave as you and your new husband depart at the end of the night.

❀ Even your ring bearer's pillow and flower girl's basket can tie into the theme of your wedding. Trade the traditional white satin pillow and basket for accessories made out of velvets in deep, rich colors with gold cording and tassels.

❀ Travel to your reception in style. Julie and her father were driven down Main Street in a horse-drawn carriage. If you want to feel like Cinderella on your wedding day, rent a coach and request a team of four white horses to pull it.

CHAPTER TWO

An Asian Dream Wedding

ALICIA AND BENJAMIN'S STORY was a modern-day fairy tale right from the start. They were neighbors growing up, and both were raised by families with tremendous pride in their Chinese American backgrounds. Frequently brought together by their parents' social nights of cooking and company, the two became fast friends. They played together until the day Alicia's family moved to California, and the two inevitably lost touch.

From a young age Alicia was independent and strong-willed—very similar to Disney's Mulan. As she grew up, her drive propelled her through many successes in school and later, in her career. Twelve years after moving to California, Alicia's company transferred her to New York City. She was reluctant to leave her loved ones behind, but she bravely faced the transition and set off on a new adventure.

Imagine her surprise when, crossing Fifth Avenue on the first day of her new job, she saw a familiar face. It was Benjamin—who swears to this day that he had never forgotten her, despite the time and distance that had

separated them. Having already lived in New York for several years, Benjamin was well-versed in the ways of big-city life. He gave Alicia her own grand tour of the Big Apple, and, within a year, proposed; they would never be parted again.

When we met Alicia and Benjamin, we could see that they were full of life and vigor, and ready to commence their happily-ever-after. They wanted a party that would celebrate all aspects of their relationship—from their childhood beginnings to their serendipitous reunion. According to an ancient East Asian legend they loved, an invisible red string is

Printed Materials

HAVING YOUR PRINTED MATERIALS correlate with one another is a fabulous touch that will create continuity throughout your wedding. Your printed materials can include (but are not limited to):

"SAVE-THE-DATE" CARDS

INVITATIONS, INCLUDING RSVP CARDS, DIRECTIONS, AND ENVELOPES

PROGRAMS

ESCORT CARDS

PLACE CARDS

MENU CARDS

FAVOR NOTES

Once you've chosen the colors you'd like to use for your printed materials (they should match the colors of your wedding), select a font that fits your personality and your wedding's style. A logo can be used on your materials to tie them together and create a finishing touch. Many couples select a beautifully designed monogram, or a symbol that has an important meaning. For Alicia and Benjamin, an Asian emblem was printed on the invitations, the tops of the programs, the escort cards, and the favor tags.

tied around the ankles of men and women who are destined to be soul mates. The legend held that, regardless of time, place, or circumstance, the two would be reunited and that, although the thread might stretch or get tangled, it would never break.

To propose to Alicia, Benjamin had taken her to the same intersection where he had spotted her on her first day of work in the city, and he presented her with an engagement ring in a box tied with—what else?—a red string. With the intention of making their wedding day just as meaningful as their past, Benjamin and Alicia decided to marry in the city that had brought them back together.

We were delighted when they expressed an interest in making their culture a prominent part of their wedding. It became the driving design direction, but just like their story, it had to have a special twist! Alicia—trendy, fashionable, and never seen without heels—wanted their wedding to be chic and a bit atypical of the traditional Chinese celebrations they were accustomed to. Her ceremony would have to be a blend of cherished custom and sleek modernity.

Such a specifically designed wedding required a venue that would be chosen with the utmost care. Alicia and Benjamin decided on the luxurious Buddakan restaurant in New York City's hip Chelsea area. The acclaimed metropolitan hot spot was perfectly compatible with Alicia's trendsetter personality, and

Buddakan's famed cuisine was well-matched with the tastes of the Asian-American couple. But most of all, the beautifully-appointed, palatial atmosphere of the dining room would make a fantastic celebration space—so fantastic that we decided to set all of the stages of their wedding there.

Alicia and Benjamin used their Save-the-Date cards to give guests a hint of what the celebration would be like. On paneled red four-by-six-inch cards with white insets, simple gold-and-black embossing elegantly proclaimed that "Alicia and Benjamin are Tying the Knot! Please Save the Date." Each card was tied with a thin red string. These cards effectively introduced the wedding's color scheme and also referenced the significance of Chinese culture in the couple's relationship.

The invitations carried on the same theme. Each card was backed by a piece of quarter-inch-thick board, and wrapped in a piece of red paper with a gold print of soft flowers and beautifully drawn Chinese dragons. All the invitation materials were placed in custom red silk dupioni boxes tied with red satin ribbons. Each beautiful box was then wrapped in red paper, addressed in gold ink, and mailed with postage stamps featuring Asian flowers.

Invitations

SEND INVITES OUT about two to three months before the wedding date, and have fun creating them. Invitations should set the tone of your wedding and include all the pertinent information:

YOUR NAMES

WHO IS HOSTING

DATE AND TIME

LOCATION

"RECEPTION TO FOLLOW"

RSVP DATE WITH RESPONSE CARD AND SELF-ADDRESSED, STAMPED ENVELOPE

ATTIRE

YOUR RETURN ADDRESS ON THE MAILING ENVELOPE

The layout and the wording can be adapted to match your wedding style. For example:

Formal

MR. AND MRS. DAVID WELLNER
INVITE YOU TO THE WEDDING CEREMONY
OF THEIR DAUGHTER

Alicia Rachel
To
Benjamin Howard

SON OF
MR. AND MRS. GLENN HUGHES

ON SATURDAY, THE ELEVENTH OF JULY,
TWO THOUSAND AND NINE

AT SIX IN THE EVENING

BUDDAKAN

NEW YORK, NEW YORK
RECEPTION IMMEDIATELY FOLLOWING
BLACK TIE

Informal

With Joy in Our Hearts,

Alicia Wellner

And

Benjamin Hughes

Request the pleasure of your presence
At their wedding celebration

Saturday, the eleventh of July
Two thousand and nine
Six o'clock in the evening

Buddakan
New York, New York

Reception immediately following
Black Tie Optional

- An RSVP/reply card

- A stamped reply-card envelope, pre-addressed to whomever will be receiving and tallying guest count (the parents of the bride, the wedding host, or the bride herself).

- A direction card detailing how guests can travel to your ceremony and reception location. Include directions from the nearest airport and train stations, and from major hotels nearby. Offer a variety of ways to access your venues.

- A reception card. If your ceremony and reception are in two different locations, insert a separate card directing guests to your party location. Remember, the formal invite applies only to your ceremony.

- Hotel accommodations. A list of nearby hotels for travelers and guests unfamiliar with the area is necessary to help them make arrangements. Speak with the nearby hotels to set up "room blocks" with special rates for your guests. (When a hotel knows your wedding will bring in a good deal of business, they may give you a discounted rate per room and ensure that the rooms are near each other.)

- If your wedding is a multi-day affair, a brief itinerary should be included as well.

When the day finally came, Benjamin and Alicia's wedding attendees entered through Buddakan's great wooden doors, and were guided by ushers in black-and-red kimonos down a candlelit hallway. On their way to their seats, the guests descended a pair of grand staircases that flanked an elaborately decorated landing where Alicia and Benjamin would exchange their vows.

On each side of the landing, a large gold urn held towering arrangements of vibrant ginger, tall red and black grasses, soft dripping moss, and glossy black bamboo poles adorned with red fabric lanterns. To give the urns height and to add another modern element, we chose to use mirrored rectangular pedestals. The mirrors were hand-painted with black branches, the

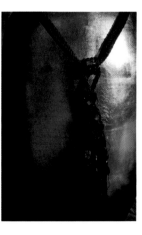

tips of which were bedecked with purple silk orchids. Votive candles were placed on each step, and clusters of Asian parasols were positioned at the bottom of the stairs. An aisle separated the guest seating into two sections, and the red runner featured a hand-painted design of black bamboo with larger corner designs of leaves and gold emblems.

For the ceremony programs, we wanted to continue with the Asian style of Alicia and Benjamin's wedding, so we used white card stock to create flat paper fans with scalloped tops, and printed them with the same floral pattern and Asian emblem that were used on the invitations. The fan handles were made of black bamboo, and red tassels with gold clasps were looped around each one.

TUTERA TIP:

If a canopy (or chuppah) is to be implemented in a ceremony, there are a couple of things to consider. If it is going to be carried, it will need to be lightweight and simply fashioned. If it's going to be grounded, you can do just about anything with decorations. Lights, flowers, or branches can be dangled, draped, strung up, or wound along the poles and around the canopy. We often go with a lightweight white fabric, but we've also used deep-hued velvety fabrics for a rustic look. Custom canopy designers often have Web sites you can browse for examples, and they can work with you and your budget to achieve a variety of different looks.

Programs

CEREMONY PROGRAMS, like your invitations, should reflect the style of your wedding. Many programs can be made using the same materials and designs as your invitations. If your wedding is a formal event, it's appropriate to have a neat, sophisticated program on each seat, but if it's a more stylized or casual wedding, you can be as creative as you like!

Regardless of what form it takes, your program should include, at minimum, text about the bride and groom, the list of names of those involved in the processional (with a description of the music accompanying them), the order of the ceremony events, the recessional music, and a thank-you to the guests and/or parents from the bride and groom. If you have additional space, or if you're opting for a booklet, it's also nice to designate a section to tell a little about the venue. You may want to add famous quotes, verses of poetry, song lyrics, a memorial tribute to deceased loved ones, or a section on wedding traditions you may be performing. At the end of your acknowledgments, include signatures from the bride and the groom.

$\mathcal{F}$ashion by Kirstie Kelly

THE EXOTIC EAST MEETS THE MODERN WEST in a formal restaurant wedding with vibrant Asian accents. We're seeing red—well, only as the uniting color for the reception—which creates a rich, winter-like atmosphere. Traditionally, red is the essential color in Chinese weddings. However, cultural fusion can be created by pairing a western bridal gown with a red sash and surrounding the bride with a bevy of red bridesmaid gowns.

For more intimate weddings like Alicia and Benjamin's, it's a good idea to avoid ball gowns that overpower both the space and hinder the bride's movement. Fully beaded sheaths or fit-and-flare gowns, or in this case, a gown laden with English tulle and large crystals, are appropriate as long as the volume is within reasonable measure. To create a more formal atmosphere, select long bridesmaid gowns that elegantly skim the floor. Unity in color and simplicity is essential for bridesmaid gowns in a small-scale wedding so as to avoid competing with the wedding's overall décor.

Alicia chose to wear a gown from the Disney Bridal Snow White collection. The A-line duchess satin gown was a perfect choice for her tall, slender frame, and the understated rouching and pleating on the empire

bodice provided just the right amount of detail. Crystal accents and a red sash were the finishing touches to a gown that looked both traditional and modern— with a splash of Eastern flavor. For her bridesmaids, Alicia selected mermaid-cut gowns from the Snow White Maidens collection. The dresses were made of ruby red taffeta with sweet and sophisticated scoop necklines. The contrasting black empire waistbands echoed the bride's sash, and the streamlined cut of the dresses enabled the ladies to move about the reception with ease. The rich red also suited the coloring of the bridesmaids, who were all brunettes, and it blended seamlessly with the design of the wedding.

Such a boldly colored wedding needed correspondingly dramatic flowers. For Alicia, we designed a bridal bouquet using white orchids, red roses, purple lisianthus, fuchsia phalaenopsis orchids, trailing jasmine, and gold ming fern. The stems were wrapped in red and gold paper and finished with a large beaded tassel. The shape of Alicia's bouquet was what made it truly unique—it was asymmetrical and curved, with orchid blossoms trailing down past the base of the handle. The bridesmaids' bouquets were similar, but they were smaller and composed entirely of blue and purple flowers.

Benjamin and Alicia's ceremony was just as touching as their real-life fairy tale. Their officiant, a longtime friend of Benjamin's family, incorporated the couple's history—and the red string of destiny—into the ceremony. Afterwards, the bride and groom and all their guests ascended the staircases for a cocktail reception.

Escort Cards

FOR FORMAL WEDDINGS, we love to have escort cards for each guest. They require time and thought, but they provide a very special touch for dinner receptions, and help in directing your guests as to where they should sit.

Escort cards should be placed in alphabetical order on a table in front of the entranceway to your reception. Guests choose their name cards to discover their table number. The goal is to make the guests feel welcome, expected, and appreciated, while offering convenient assistance in finding the spot where they should be sitting. For ease of creation and execution both, we recommend keeping escort cards simple!

For Buddakan's marble bar, we created arrangements of red and black bamboo stems, moss, and purple orchids, and set them in clear cylindrical vases. Next to each large arrangement, we placed a smaller one in a metallic red vase. A gold tassel was strung around the neck of each vase.

As the ceremony space was transformed into the dinner space, waiters in kimonos served edamame dumplings with shallot-Sauternes broth; tuna spring rolls with crisp shallots and ponzu; and lettuce cups with beef, puffed rice, and pickled tomato salad. Guests were served two specialty drinks that Alicia and Benjamin had selected based on flavors they liked and the colors of their wedding. The first, called Destiny, was a sunny concoction that included passion fruit liqueur, apple, fresh berries, and Prosecco. The second, called Fate, was a reddish mix of elderflower, pineapple, and Prosecco, served in a glass rimmed with edible gold.

When it was time for the reception to begin, the guests were directed back toward the staircase, where they found a table arranged with escort cards. The table was draped in Asian-themed black linen printed with detailed images of dragons, and the surface was covered with red rose petals. Each card was held by a gleaming black ceramic candleholder in the shape of a lotus flower and bore a simplified version of the familiar red trim, in addition to Alicia and Benjamin's emblem. The candleholders later became favors for guests to take home.

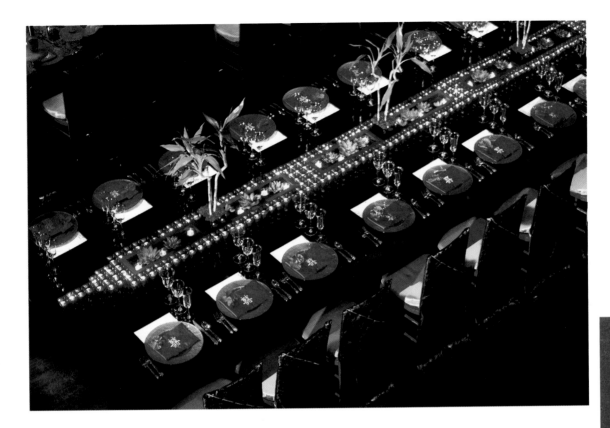

At this point, the couple and their party returned downstairs to discover a brand-new scene—an inviting Asian banquet, complete with a long dinner table fit for an emperor's palace. Alicia and Benjamin were enthralled by the profusion of color and light. Hundreds of tea-light candles, glowing in square red votives, made a spectacular, unusual table runner. Amid the candles, black cast-iron water troughs were filled with floating purple lotus flowers and glass-enclosed white candles. Several arrangements

of twisting bamboo stems and red moss were positioned at intervals along the table to complete the look.

Eleven people sat on each side of the long dining table, with Alicia and Benjamin in the middle. The backs of the chairs were covered with satin fabric in an elegant Asian print. Because of the shape of the room, we needed additional tables at which to seat all of Alicia and Benjamin's guests, so we took advantage of a long built-in bench that ran along one wall and positioned three rectangular tables in front of it.

TUTERA TIP:
With any wedding, it's important to do two things—make sure the ceremony can be seen, and make sure the ceremony can be heard. So, use microphones for bride, groom, and officiant unless you are having a very small wedding and everyone has practiced projecting their voices. Small wireless microphones are great for the groom and officiant, but you don't want to clip any devices to a bridal dress, no matter how discreet. Microphones can easily be suspended above the ceremony from an archway or canopy.

with gold flatware. Three gold-rimmed clear glasses (for champagne, water, and wine) were arranged in a straight line—as opposed to the traditional cluster—at the head of each setting. A personalized menu card was slipped underneath the top of each napkin plate, just barely revealing the couple's names and enticing each guest to learn more about the culinary delights they would soon experience.

Alicia and Benjamin had both grown up in families that loved to cook and share their passion for food, so the couple chose their menu based on their favorite dishes and the strong suits of Buddakan's chefs. For appetizers, guests were served crispy calamari salad; scallion pancakes with braised beef short rib and shaved green apple; chilled udon noodles with lime sorbet and peanut sauce; and Asian stir-fry with pine nuts and garlic chips. Then the servers brought out two main courses: charred fillet of beef with wonton crisps and mustard sauce, and sweet and crispy jumbo shrimp with citrus salad and radish.

When decorating side tables, we always like to give them a little something extra. The easiest way to give a simple table a jolt of pizzazz is to provide it with layers of height, shape, and depth. For Alicia and Benjamin's side tables, we began with black satin tablecloths and magenta runners. A few of the red square votives were interspersed among a series of pagoda-shaped metal votives, and bamboo arrangements identical to those on the main table gave the centerpiece height and flair.

Regardless of which table the guests were assigned to, all would have the same place settings. We started each place setting with a hammered copper charger plate. Atop each charger lay a folded red napkin with the Chinese characters for "Double Happiness" custom-embroidered in the center. We set a purple orchid blossom on the corner of each napkin, and each setting was framed

Last, but not least, the desserts arrived. Guests had a choice between a delectable blood-orange sorbet and Buddakan's famous Crying Chocolate dish—a malted chocolate ganache with coffee ice cream. As if that weren't enough, Alicia and Benjamin's cake was one of the most outstanding parts of their wedding. Designed by hand and covered with sculpted fondant, the spectacular dessert was a four-tiered cake in the shape of a Chinese pagoda.

At the end of the evening, a hostess distributed satchels of red rose petals to the couple's guests so that they could shower Alicia and Benjamin with love as they departed for their new life together. After living separate lives that had been intermittently woven together, Alicia and Benjamin were tied by the bonds of marriage—and a strong red string.

Menu Cards

Menu cards can be as simple or as detailed as you'd like them to be. You can personalize them and include detailed descriptions of each course along with its wine pairings, or you can opt for a straightforward outline of the meal. However, regardless of the wording, each guest should always get his or her own. Don't print just one or two and place them in the middle of the table. Your guests might feel as if they are at a diner!

Here is an example of what a menu card might look like:

Menu

ALICIA AND BENJAMIN'S WEDDING

SATURDAY, JULY 11, 2009

BUDDAKAN
NEW YORK CITY

APPETIZER
Crispy calamari salad
Scallion pancakes
Chilled udon noodles
Asian stir fry

SALAD
Heirloom tomato salad
with goat cheese and aged balsamic vinegar

MAIN COURSE
Charred fillet of beef
Sweet-and-crispy jumbo shrimp

DESSERT
Vanilla bean wedding cake
Blood-orange sorbet
Crying Chocolate

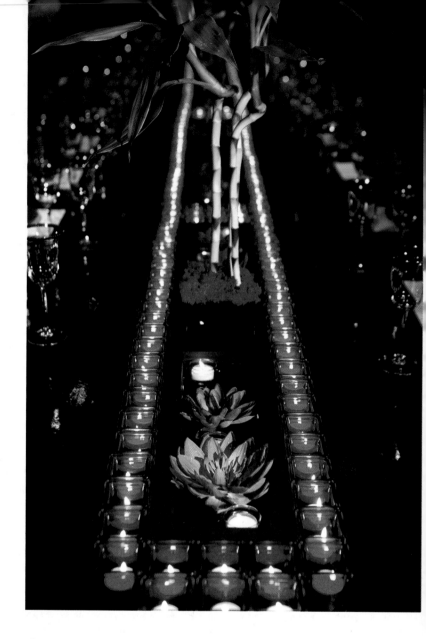

OVERVIEW:

FASHION:

The bride wore an A-line duchess satin gown from the Disney Bridal Snow White collection. The bodice was lightly rouched and pleated, and the neckline sparkled with crystal accents. A rich red sash tied at the waist gave the bride's look a hint of color.

The bridesmaids wore mermaid-cut red taffeta gowns from the Snow White Maidens collection.

INVITATION:

Paneled red cards made of thick red ribbed card stock were backed by quarter-inch-thick board and wrapped in red paper printed with gold flowers and Chinese dragons. The gold script text was embossed and set off by a red Asian emblem.

COLOR SWATCHES/ FLORAL GUIDE:

COLORS: red, black, green, purple, gold, and fuchsia

FLOWERS: bamboo stems, purple and white lisianthus, fuschia and white phalaenopsis orchids, jasmine, black manzanita branches, gold ming fern, green and red moss, purple lotus, and ginger

MENU:

APPETIZER

Crispy calamari salad

Scallion pancakes

Chilled udon noodles

Asian stir fry

SALAD

Heirloom tomato salad
with goat cheese and aged
balsamic vinegar

MAIN COURSE

Charred fillet of beef

Sweet-and-crispy jumbo shrimp

DESSERT

Vanilla bean wedding cake

Blood-orange sorbet

Crying Chocolate

SPECIALTY DRINK: FATE

Elderflower liqueur

Fresh pineapple juice

Prosecco

Shake equal parts in a mixer with ice and pour.
Rim each martini glass with edible gold by dipping
the edge of each glass in water, and then into a tray
of gold flakes.

MUSIC SUGGESTIONS:

FIRST DANCE

"Reflection" Instrumental
– From *Mulan*

"From This Moment" – Shania Twain

FATHER-DAUGHTER DANCE

"Lean on Me" – Bill Withers

"Unforgettable" – Nat King Cole

MOTHER-SON DANCE

"I'm Your Angel" – Céline Dion

"I Hope You Dance"
– Lee Ann Womack

DISNEY TOUCHES: *Mulan*

※ For many couples, their culture is an important part of their wedding. Like Mulan, Alicia and Benjamin felt a strong loyalty to their Chinese heritage and traditions. They chose to incorporate traditional Chinese elements into the design of their printed materials. You might choose to feature a cricket like Cri-Kee on your thank-you notes and escort cards.

※ Floral arrangements can really help to tie a concept together and add a personal touch to a wedding. Select flowers that suit your personality and complement your style. A bridal bouquet made of lotus flowers would certainly suit Mulan.

※ It's important to make your ceremony space intimate and striking, but not so striking that it detracts from the bridal couple. We used urns, bamboo, and lanterns to frame the landing at Buddakan, but you might choose to frame your ceremony space with red guardian dragons that resemble Mushu.

※ Regardless of your budget, your wedding cake can be made to reflect the theme of your wedding. Alicia and Benjamin chose a four-tiered pagoda with intricate fondant work. If price is not an issue and Mulan is your favorite Disney heroine, you could request an elaborate cake in the shape of the Emperor's Palace. However, if you're looking to spend more sparingly, you could opt for a simple round cake emblazoned with the Emperor's medallion in royal icing.

※ Make a statement with your escort cards! We placed the escort cards for Alicia and Benjamin's wedding on ceramic lotus-flower candleholders that also became guest favors. A *Mulan*-inspired escort card could sit atop a dragon-shaped incense burner like the one Fa Zhou uses to pray for his daughter.

CHAPTER THREE

An Indian Dream Wedding

FEW THINGS EXHIBIT the most enduring aspects of a given culture as a wedding does. A couple's heritage can play a significant role in their relationship, and it can often determine which aspects of life they hold most dear. The histories and traditions of foreign countries can become even more meaningful when woven throughout a day as important as a wedding. While many couples may want modern, trendy weddings, there are some whose tastes are strongly associated with the places their ancestors came from. For these brides and grooms, there is something magical about the vitality of cherished rituals, and nothing is more important than incorporating those rituals into their wedding celebrations.

Nisha and Sameer were college sweethearts. Their story began when they met on the first day of orientation, and it wasn't long before they discovered that they had a lot in common. They were both of Indian descent, and they shared strong ties to their ethnic backgrounds. They also shared an interest in science; she was a biology student and he was an engineer. As their college years went by, the two became incredibly well-versed in their respective

fields—and they also grew closer to each other. Nisha and Sameer stayed together through grad school, and none of their friends or family was surprised when the couple announced that they were getting married.

Nisha and Sameer had a traditional Indian wedding ceremony in their home city of Mumbai, where they celebrated with their relatives and honored their ancestry. Yet, having lived so much of their lives in the

United States, they longed for a wedding that would include their American friends. They came to us with the hope of planning a grand celebration that would bring their friends and family together, while honoring their heritage at the same time.

When the couple met with us for their initial consultation, we were struck by their devotion to each other. We also couldn't help noticing Nisha's resemblance to a certain spirited princess: Jasmine, from Disney's *Aladdin*. The bride-to-be had Jasmine's beautiful, glossy black hair, striking eyes, and radiant skin. Not to mention the fact that she was driven and incredibly smart! Sameer felt wonderfully lucky to have found his lovely princess, and he knew that he couldn't have wished for a more perfect partner—even if he had had a genie in a magic lamp!

When we set about planning their wedding, we had many factors to take into consideration. Indian weddings are some of the most beautiful celebrations in the world. They are characterized by exotic foods, jubilant dancing, stunning traditional attire, and an astounding use of color. In Indian culture, the brighter a wedding's colors are, the more celebratory the occasion is, so we created an exhilarating palette of orange, peach, fuchsia, violet, pale yellow, and green. Such vivid colors would paint Nisha and Sameer's wedding with life, love, and the flavors of India.

Traditionally, Indian weddings are not small affairs. In fact, Nisha and Sameer planned to have six hundred guests. They explained that weddings in their culture emphasize the union of two families. Both of their family trees had many, many branches, and since family was important to both the bride and the groom, it was essential to include everyone. The couple also reasoned that a gathering of this many people required an extended celebration, so they decided to plan two days of wedding events for their friends and family to enjoy.

A two-day, grand-scale wedding required a grand-scale invitation. Each guest received a burgundy velvet envelope with a gold paisley design, wrapped with a chain of jingling medallions. The invitations themselves were printed on orange paper backed with burgundy card stock. Traditional *mehndi* designs— typically drawn on the bride's hands and feet

with henna—surrounded the event details. Nisha and Sameer's series of wedding events would include a day-long welcome celebration and a grand wedding feast the following day at the landmark National Building Museum in Washington, D.C.

Since it is customary for the groom's family to host the initial event, the welcoming party was held at the home of Sameer's family in Maryland. The house was situated on a large piece of property, so we chose to host the guests in a tent. Upon arriving, Nisha and Sameer's guests entered a tented foyer that had been decorated with spheres of deep burgundy and

bright pink carnations, and orange and yellow roses. Ribbons imported from India rained down from the arrangements, which had been suspended from the ceiling. Water trickled from a stone fountain in a long reflecting pool, which was inspired by the Taj Mahal's famed gardens, and purple button mums and bright rose petals floated on every tier of the fountain. The floating rose petals were meant to symbolize the traditional Indian *Jalastnchana* ritual, or "blessing of the couple," during which the parents of the bride and groom bless the wedded couple by dipping a rose in water and sprinkling the water over them.

Inside the tent, dramatic swags of bright chiffon billowed from the ceiling. We surrounded the tent poles with green bamboo shoots and palm fronds to create the look of palm trees, effectively concealing the tent's structure. Tablecloths of bright magenta satin alternating with gold pin-tuck taffeta covered sixty round tables, and gold Chiavari chairs with brightly colored cushions completed

the look. All together, the fabrics created an opulent impression that was traditional and vivacious at the same time.

On top of each table, collections of lanterns and mosaic candleholders were interspersed among gold bowls overflowing with red and peach roses, purple button mums, lemons, limes, grapes, and kiwis. The delicious aroma of exotic foods wafted through the air from food stations set up around the room. These canopied stations were decorated with colorful and asymmetrical swaths of fabric and braided trim, giving them the look of an extravagant Indian marketplace. At each station, we hung chalkboards displaying lists of the foods served within. The name of each dish was written in both Hindi and in English so that guests from India and the U.S. could easily find their favorite foods.

TUTERA TIP:
Make your wedding a night to remember! Captivate your guests by providing some kind of entertainment. This may come in the form of music, dancing, a dramatic performance, a slide show, or a make-your-own sundae bar.

An additional station was created for entertainment. To incorporate the pre-marriage mehndi ritual, during which the bride's hands and feet are decorated with henna, we designed an area where Indian henna artists would do just that. We created an open-air structure and draped it with fabrics and orange and green flower garlands. These garlands were meant to reflect the traditional ceremony of the *Jaimala*, the "exchange of garlands," during which the couple exchange garlands as a gesture of acceptance of one another and a pledge to respect one another as partners.

To make the henna station look plush and inviting, we piled a large bed with colorful silk pillows upon which Nisha and her guests could lounge while the painters worked their magic. The guests had their own hands and feet painted, too, and took turns studying Nisha's beautiful swirling designs trying to find a hidden message; the name of the groom is traditionally woven into the bride's mehndi, and the groom is later tasked with finding it.

*D*isc Jockeys

DISC JOCKEYS ARE AN EXCELLENT CHOICE FOR ENTERTAINMENT, and they are often much less expensive than live entertainment. In fact, many brides lean toward using deejays because the playlist can be specifically customized to suit the couple's wishes. For their wedding, Nisha and Sameer hired a specialty deejay who dressed in Indian clothes and provided all the traditional songs that the couple wanted to hear. If you plan to hire a deejay, you should research several individuals to learn about their personalities, styles, and abilities. Meet with them, and discuss your needs and wishes for your wedding, and if possible, watch them in action. Once you've made your choice, spend time developing your playlist. This will ensure that the deejay has a plan to keep the rhythm of the party tailored to your personal tastes.

After guests had eaten their fill of delicious Indian food, they danced to the songs played by an Indian deejay. Nisha and Sameer danced late into the night, even though they knew that an even bigger celebration awaited them the next day!

For the day of Nisha and Sameer's main celebration, it was our goal to transform D.C.'s National Building Museum into a palace. The inspiration for the reception was the tale of Emperor Shah Jahan, who had the Taj Mahal built as a mausoleum for his beloved wife. The emperor had requested that the structure be built with white marble, inlaid with semi-precious stones, and it was this regal look that served as the spark for our design concept.

Beginning with the blank canvas of the National Building Museum's Great Hall, we set out to create an environment characterized by lustrous jewel tones. Rich hues such as ruby, sapphire, amethyst, garnet, and gold were used to give the space a feeling of luxury, prominence, and splendor.

It was also important that we incorporate traditional Indian elements into the décor. As guests stepped into the cocktail area, they encountered a pair of peacocks facing each other atop a pyramid of gilded stone urns. Peacocks are a symbol of wealth and elegance in India, because ancient kings would keep the exotic birds in their gardens and invite guests to marvel at the splendor of their incredible feathers. Peacocks are also used in Indian stories, songs, and poems, as symbols of beauty and poise. The perfectly plumed birds were set upon a vibrant arrangement that featured tall stalks of wheat, one of India's most abundant resources.

Throughout the cocktail hour, butlers dressed in traditional *sherwanis* offered guests a specialty drink called Bombay Breeze. The light and sweet concoction was served in pink-patterned tea glasses garnished with

blood orange slices and mint leaves. The other specialty drink was a light pink, vodka-infused lemonade rimmed with sugar crystals and garnished with a fresh raspberry and a lemon twist. It was aptly named Arabian Nights, in honor of Colva Beach, a vacation spot on the Arabian Sea where the bride and groom planned to take their honeymoon.

When it was time to move into the reception area, the guests encountered an escort card table draped in burgundy and orange silk. Floral garlands connected three gold candelabra that sat atop the table, and in the center, a double candelabra served as the base for an arrangement of red gloriosa, orange

Live Music

WHETHER IT'S SALSA OR SWING, a twenty-piece band or a four-piece ensemble, live music has the ability to invigorate a room, heighten the energy level of the guests, and keep a party in motion for the duration of your celebration. Before you set out to find a band, you must first identify the style of music you want for your event. Nisha and Sameer wanted both classical and modern Indian music, ranging from Bhangra to Bollywood.

When you undertake the task of choosing a band, be sure to hear them live before you sign them. CDs and DVDs can give you a good sense of a band's repertoire, but a group's performance style is something that can really only be experienced in person. Discuss appropriate attire with your band leader, create a playlist with him or her, and ask for references. Also be sure to share your wedding timeline with your bandleader, and make sure that the band's sound, stage, and lighting requirements are in compliance with your venue. Last, make sure to have a platform or stage for your band to perform on. You and your guests should be able to see and interact with the band!

From a platform stage, an authentic Indian band performed lively, traditional music. Since Indian dances are performed as an expression of joy, the dance floor was sure to be full that night.

A mixture of long and round tables surrounded the dance floor. They were draped in full-length pink satin imported from India and accompanied by golden Chiavari chairs with pink and orange cushions. On each table, golden flower stands held elevated arrangements of red gloriosa, orange and green ranunculus, deep pink phalaenopsis orchids, peach and pink roses, bright pink bouvardia, green hydrangeas, and blue vandal orchids. Strands of pink crystals interspersed with orange teardrops hung from the spherical

ranunculus, button mums, and yellow and orange roses. The name cards were arranged in front of gold bowls filled with roses, bouvardia, and hydrangeas. A magenta curtain concealed the reception area from view, and when the curtains were finally pulled back, an opulent Indian paradise was unveiled.

The room was dressed for an imperial event. From the Great Hall's two-story archways we hung tapestries of magenta and orange fabric that spanned from ceiling to floor. The building's famous Corinthian columns were up-lit with pink and orange lights, and the dance floor in the center of the hall glowed with the same energetic tones.

arrangements. For the place settings, we chose gold-rimmed goblets, gilded charger plates, and golden flatware. Handmade silk napkins embroidered with Sameer's family crest were tucked into napkin rings that came from the couple's home city of Mumbai.

In order to make the bridal couple feel like Indian royalty, we constructed a platform for their sweetheart table that would allow them to look out on the reception as they dined. Atop the platform, their table was set underneath a wooden gazebo draped with orange and pink fabrics. A crystal chandelier was suspended from the gazebo, giving the table a romantic glow, and a thick garland of flowers was wrapped around the tabletop, trailing down the front of the table, and circling the hem of the table skirt.

Nisha and Sameer wanted their guests to feel as though they were dining in India, so we created an authentic menu that incorporated the couple's favorite dishes and flavors. Courses of prawns, kebabs in tamarind-mint sauce, rack of lamb, and Goan fish curry stimulated the guests' tastebuds and transported them to Southern Asia. For dessert, the partygoers dined on delicious coconut confections spiced with fresh cardamom, and Gulab Jamun, a pastry made with rosewater syrup.

The finale of the meal was an incredible, towering wedding cake that fit perfectly with the theme of the celebration. Since there are seven steps in an Indian couple's wedding vows and the number seven is considered to be good luck, Nisha and Sameer's cake had seven magnificent tiers. Each of these was covered in bright pink fondant and decorated with intricate Indian designs that resembled the embellishments on an ornate sari. The cake was accented with brightly colored flowers and set on a table strewn with pink flower petals. The overall effect was truly breathtaking.

Accompanying the cake service, the waiters presented each guest with a token of thanks from Nisha and Sameer. Beaded ring boxes, sent by the bride's family in India, would serve as reminders of the wonderful evening the guests had shared with the bride and groom.

Once the cake was served and eaten, Nisha and Sameer hit the dance floor to celebrate their marriage in song and dance. Guests clothed in glittering fabrics joined the festivities, filling the room with energy. The revelers rejoiced in their Indian palace until the late hours of the night, celebrating a couple who were sure to preserve their culture's traditions and also create some of their own.

Overview:

Fashion:

For the welcome celebration, Nisha wore a white silk sari with gold embroidery. The following evening, she wore a traditional red sari.

Invitation:

Accented with traditional mehndi designs, the invitations were printed on orange paper backed by burgundy card stock. Each invitation was sent in a burgundy velvet envelope wrapped in a chain of medallions.

Color Swatches/ Floral Guide

COLORS: pink, purple, peach, light yellow, deep orange, green, gold, red

FLOWERS: red gloriosa; orange and green ranunculus; pink phalaenopsis orchids; peach and pink roses; pink bouvardia; green hydrangeas; blue vanda orchids; green, yellow and purple button mums; burgundy and pink carnations

Specialty drink: Arabian Nights

Sugar

2 oz. raspberry vodka

2 oz. pink lemonade

Fresh raspberry and lemon twist for garnish

Coat rim of a glass with sugar. Combine the vodka and pink lemonade in a shaker with ice. Shake and strain into glass. Garnish with raspberry and lemon twist.

MENU:

STARTERS

Prawns with minted pea puree and Aloo Tikki: grilled potato cakes with mango chutney

Lamb, swordfish, and vegetable kebabs with tamarind mint sauce and apricot chutney

MAIN COURSE

Adraki Chaap: rack of lamb with ginger and rum, and braised cabbage with scallions and coriander

Goan fish curry with chilies, peppers, and caramelized onions in saffron coconut milk broth

DESSERT

Gulab Jamun: pastry puffs with sweet cardamom and rosewater syrup

Coconut Burfi: sweet coconut confections with fresh cardamom

MUSIC SUGGESTIONS:

FIRST DANCE

"A Whole New World" – from *Aladdin*

"Let's Stay Together" – Al Green

FATHER-DAUGHTER DANCE

"Can You Feel the Love Tonight?" – Elton John

"My Girl" – The Temptations

MOTHER-SON DANCE

"Candle on the Water" – from *Pete's Dragon*

"What a Wonderful World" – Louis Armstrong

FAVOR:

Nisha and Sameer's guests received beaded ring boxes sent from India by Nisha's family.

DISNEY TOUCHES: *Aladdin*

 A wedding is a celebration of a shared wish coming true. So what would an *Aladdin*-inspired wedding be without a magic lamp or two? Look for candleholders that resemble Genie's lamp and place them on your dinner tables.

 In many cases, it's difficult to bring a large number of guests to a destination wedding. But that doesn't mean that you can't bring the destination to your guests! The décor of Nisha and Sameer's wedding made their friends feel as though they were celebrating in India! If you'd like to whisk your guests away to the sultan's palace in Agrabah, decorate your venue with flowing fabrics, and create seating areas with large pillows in rich jewel tones.

 A sweetheart table is perfect for couples who want to focus on each other during their reception. If you'd like your dining experience to feel like a magic-carpet ride, have a platform constructed for your private table, and drape the platform with oriental rugs. Add a few golden tassels, and you'll have created "A Whole New World" like Aladdin and Jasmine's.

 If you are planning to serve dinner buffet-style, there's no reason not to tie the buffets into your theme. At their welcoming party, Nisha and Sameer had stands constructed to resemble an Indian marketplace. The same technique can be used to create a bazaar straight out of Agrabah.

 Incorporating animal-inspired elements, like the peacock arrangement at Nisha and Sameer's cocktail hour, can make a bold statement at your wedding. You don't have to arrive on an elephant, like Prince Ali— although you can if you want to! An *Aladdin*-inspired wedding could feature monkey-shaped placecard holders, or tiger-print charger plates and napkin rings.

CHAPTER FOUR

A Sparkle Dream Wedding

T AKING TIME TO CREATE MOMENTS of unexpected joy is what makes planning a wedding so exciting. The magic is in the details—and in the element of surprise. Jane and Matthew were a young couple about to receive the surprise of a lifetime. The bride's father, John, was giving a priceless gift to his daughter and future son-in-law: the wedding of their dreams. The couple would be exempt from all the planning—their responsibility was simply to enjoy their celebration.

Rarely does a father of the bride relish the details of wedding planning the way John did. Since Jane's childhood, he had promised his daughter that her wedding day would be the best day of her life, "just as she made every day the best of his." Jane delightfully relinquished control of her special day to allow her father the pleasure of creating a spectacular wedding that would take her breath away.

However, we did allow the bride to have some input. Jane told us that she loved "all things girlie," the color pink, white phalaenopsis orchids, roses, and diamonds. Since she was petite, feminine, and sassy, she immediately put us in mind of Disney's precocious pixie, Tinker Bell. We knew that we would have to give Jane's wedding a generous sprinkling of pixie dust and sparkle. With these elements as a foundation and John's careful guidance, we set out to create an elegant yet extravagant wedding with a modern twist. The historic Philadelphia Park Hyatt hotel would serve as the setting for a fabulously floral wedding ceremony, to be followed by a diamond-studded reception.

ceremony ballroom with sheer white fabric. Then the focus shifted to the aisle treatment. Using simple garden arbors as a base, we constructed three archways out of various shades of pink and white flowers, which were studded with diamond accents. A bevy of white and pink roses, white hydrangeas, tulips, calla lilies, and white phalaenopsis orchids adorned each archway, and crystal garlands were woven in to give the design some added sparkle. A custom aisle runner was hand-painted with the couple's monogram and was bordered by rose petals that transitioned from white, at the far end, to pink at the altar. Flower "hedges" framed both sides of the aisle and featured diamond patterns created with white and cream-colored roses. On top of each hedge, glass candleholders connected with strands of crystals held candles that would light the bride's path during the ceremony.

TUTERA TIP:

If you want flowers to be a prominent element in your wedding, but roses are too expensive, use carnations. They are much more cost-efficient and are available in just as many colors.

John told us that in her youth, Jane had always been a daydreamer. John wanted her wedding to feel like a daydream, and we decided that the best way to achieve this would be to create a floral paradise in her favorite colors: pink and white. We also knew that Jane's walk down the aisle with her father would be an incredibly important moment for both of them, so we wanted to draw attention to that aspect of the ceremony.

To create Jane's dreamlike environment, we began by draping the perimeter of the

When the day of the wedding arrived, two hundred guests were escorted to gold Chiavari chairs that had been arranged on both sides of the aisle so that they angled toward the center. Each chair was covered with sheer, champagne-colored organza, and cones filled with rose petals were tied to the back of each chair with pink ribbon. A white program card accompanied by a pink rose had been placed on each seat. A musical ensemble played soft music, cuing a hostess to untie a garland of white roses and hydrangeas that roped off the aisle.

While Jane and John waited behind the closed doors of the ballroom, the four bridesmaids came down the aisle in cappuccino-colored floor-length gowns. They carried bouquets made of white calla lilies affixed with faux diamond accents, and the stems were wrapped with white fabric, encircled with bands of faux diamonds, and embellished with faux diamond-studded buckles.

Finally, the doors of the ballroom were opened, and Jane beamed as she took in the overwhelming sight of her dream wedding ceremony. She wore a strapless, mermaid-cut gown made of white satin with a perfectly fitted bodice and a crystal-beaded neckline. With a chapel-length veil that grazed the floor, Jane was just as much a vision as her surroundings. Her round bridal bouquet was composed entirely of

THE WEDDING CEREMONY OF

Jane Elizabeth Fisher
to
Matthew Wheeler Twan

SATURDAY, THE TWENTIETH OF SEPTEMBER
TWO THOUSAND AND EIGHT
AT SEVEN O'CLOCK IN THE EVENING
THE RAINBOW ROOM

Parents of the Bride		Parents of the Groom
John and Ronni Fisher		David and
		the late Ellen Twan
Maid of Honor	PROCESSIONAL	
Alexandra Rosloff	CIRCLING	Best Man
	FAMILY BLESSING	David Twan
Bridesmaids	FIRST CUP OF WINE	
Cathy Glosser	EXCHANGING OF RINGS	Groomsmen
Rachel Goodman	AND RABBI'S REMARKS	Joshua Fogel
Linda Hoffman		Richard Glosser
Susan Hyman	SECOND CUP OF WINE	David Twan Jr.
Randi Levitch	RECESSIONAL	Jonathan Hyman
Lauren Liles		Joshua Korin
Tiffany Weinstraub		Douglas Levitch
		Daniel Mond
Junior Bridesmaids		
Hannah Glosser	Officiate	
Evangeline Van Houten	Rabbi Lisa Grushcow	
		Ushers
Flower Girl	Singing During the Ketubah Signing	
Isabelle Hyman	"Dodi L" Steven Ralston	
Ring Bearer	Singing Before	
Zachary Lowe		

Kindly reply by
the twentieth of August

M _____

_____ accepts _____ regrets

Brooklyn, New York 11217

Mr. and Mrs. John and Ronni Fisher
would be delighted if you would join them
at the marriage of their daughter

Jane Elizabeth Fisher
to
Matthew Wheeler Twan

son of

Mr. David Twan
and the late Mrs. Ellen Twan

Saturday, the twentieth of September
Two thousand and eight
at seven o'clock in the evening
The Rainbow Room, 30 Rockefeller Center
New York City

Dinner and Dancing to follow

white stephanotis flowers. The center of each flower held a faux diamond, and the full length of the bouquet handle was wrapped with faux diamonds as well.

Jane linked arms with her father and winked at him. John beamed, knowing that he had given his daughter the wedding of her dreams. He walked her down the aisle underneath the flower archways, and then Matthew and Jane exchanged their vows in front of their friends and family.

After the ceremony, the guests were ushered into the Park Hyatt's two-level

ballroom foyer for the cocktail hour. Parallel winding staircases curved down each side of the room, and a sheer curtain hung across the entrance to the dinner reception. Five-foot urns spilled over with calla lilies, and vases covered in faux diamonds sparkled on the bars. Jane and Matthew sipped a pink, rose-infused cocktail created just for their wedding. Then the lights behind the curtains changed color, the music swelled, and the guests were asked to move into the reception area; the party had begun.

Table Décor

TABLE LINENS: Linens for wedding receptions consist of an overlay and an underlay. The underlay should be a basic color that accents the colors of the wedding. The overlay can have interesting textures, beading, prints, or colors. A full-length tablecloth is 60 inches plus the size of the table. For example, a 30- inch round table would require a 90-inch tablecloth.

CHAIRS: Chairs are available in a multitude of colors and styles. They can also be decorated and customized with cushions. Chair covers—also called chair backs—can really add polish to the look of your reception.

PLACE SETTINGS: China, flatware, and stemware complete the look of your design, so it is important to select your pieces carefully. The basic items in a place setting are:

> **CHARGER PLATES:** These twelve-inch decorative plates add texture and color to each place setting. The charger plate sits underneath a dinner plate, and it is removed before dessert is served.

> **GLASSWARE:** Wine glasses, champagne flutes, and water goblets should be provided for each place setting.

> **FLATWARE:** Utensils come in a variety of materials, ranging from stainless steel to gold-plated.

> **CHINA:** Dinner plates, appetizer plates, soup bowls, salad and bread plates, dessert plates, and coffee mugs and saucers fall under the category of china. You can be consistent with one pattern or deliberately mix and match designs that complement one another.

TUTERA TIP:
Try battery-operated tapered candles if candles are not permitted in the space you have hired. You can rent them from a party supply company or purchase them online.

The ballroom was revealed, and it was a dreamland of flowers, crystal, and silver. The room had been draped with white fabric and was lit with pink lights. Strands of crystals hung from the columns. The table numbers were displayed inside imitation diamond-studded picture frames, and each place setting sparkled thanks to a crystal paperweight engraved with a guest's name.

For a party of this scale, we prefer to design a few different, but coordinating table looks, to break up the space. But variations in table shape were not enough to make this wedding a truly unique one. Eight tables were hand-crafted for Jane and Matthew's dinner reception by our team of designers. Each of the custom tables was eight feet long and covered in silver leaf. The tops and sides were inlaid with faux diamonds, and the tables were set without linens.

The remaining tables were a mix of round and long and featured three different designs. The circular tables were adorned with spherical arrangements of white roses resting in tall glass vases. Oversize faux diamonds were placed in the bottom of each vase, and large leaves of grass sprouted from each arrangement. A mirrored box served as the base for each arrangement, and the boxes were covered in white rose blossoms and surrounded with votive candles. The second

Lighting

Many brides neglect lighting because of budget constraints, but it can really make a huge impact on the mood and energy of a wedding. If you opt for a customized lighting setup, you will need a lighting technician on-site at all times to operate it, especially if you want the colors to change throughout the wedding. This can get pricey, but the effects are amazing. If you're looking for a less expensive option, we highly recommend using candles. You might want to try lighting an abundance of votive candles, pillar candles of various sizes in glass hurricanes, and/or tapered candles in candelabra. Since lighting is so versatile, it can give each area of your reception a different pace. Here are a few areas to consider for special lighting concepts:

Ceremony Aisle: Nothing sets the tone for a romantic environment better than candlelight.

Ceremony Area (Altar, Chuppah, Archway): Test the lighting before the actual wedding. You'll want to make sure that your face is not lost in shadows for the wedding pictures.

Tables: We prefer to use a warm glowing light that illuminates the entire tabletop. Spotlights can create a blind spot in the wedding photography.

Dance Floor: You don't want it to be too bright, but a dark dance floor will make your guests drowsy. When you take the floor for your first dance as a couple, request that the lights be dimmed and that a spotlight follow you around.

Stage: If you have a band, the stage must have brighter lighting than the rest of the dance floor. The musicians may also have special requirements, so be sure to check with the bandleader.

Cake Table: Consider spotlighting the cake. Place the cake table near the entrance to the dinner area, not off in a dark corner.

Walls: The perimeter of your space can be lit from above or below. Choose colors that complement your theme, and consider using gobos that project your monogram or another custom pattern.

table design featured tall glass vases of white phalaenopsis orchids, and the third involved shallow mirrored boxes containing bouquets of calla lilies.

The tables at Jane and Matthew's wedding were dressed with various styles of linen. Some tables were covered in elegant floor-length white tablecloths with faux diamond trim, and others were adorned with lacy, beaded linens. White-upholstered high-backed chairs were custom-made with faux diamond—encrusted silver buckles. A sleek silver charger plate served as the foundation for each place setting, and each

white napkin was neatly folded and secured with a round faux diamond buckle. Square-handled flatware coordinated with the clear, silver-rimmed glass goblets.

We wanted to create a very special sweetheart table for Jane and Matthew, so that they would have an intimate retreat amid the extravagance of their reception. We constructed a canopy out of sheer white organza and gathered the sides with flower arrangements. Glorious flower garlands surrounded the foot of each gathered side panel, and another lush garland curled around the front of the table. The abundant flowers on top of the table were lit by white candles. Garlands adorned the backs of the bride's and groom's chairs, making the couple feel as though they were dining in an enchanted garden.

The romantic mood of the reception was created through carefully engineered lighting. Since the bride had such an affinity for pink, the walls were lit with hues of magenta that alternated with purples and blues every thirty minutes to keep the guests in an ever-changing environment. We also used gobos—templates used to create light patterns—to project floral patterns throughout the reception area.

The final component of Jane and Matthew's lighting design was a series of trusses—structures positioned near the ceiling to hold lights that shine down from above. These are typically used to cast light on musicians, other entertainment, and dance floors. The music at Jane and Matthew's wedding was provided by a large band with a brass section, in addition to a disc jockey that played between sets. Trusses were placed around the perimeter of the dance floor in order to light the band, the deejay, and the dance floor.

The dance floor itself was white, with a decal featuring the couple's monogram. After her first dance with Matthew, Jane joined her

Wedding Cakes

THE FIRST STEP in choosing a wedding cake is finding a baker. While you're searching, keep in mind that it's important to share the baker's tastes—in both flavor and artistic style. In determining if a baker is right for you, going for a cake tasting is a must. This will allow you to meet your baker, sample several flavor options, and discuss the vision you have for your cake design. Inquire about how the baker's cakes are made, what ingredients are used, and how the cakes are kept fresh. Ask the baker for references from other brides who have used him/her in the past, and hire only a baker that you feel you can trust.

After you've selected the baker, have a follow-up conversation, to discuss in depth the details of your cake concept. Tell your baker about your wedding theme, the colors, your dress, the location, and the flowers, and ask for recommendations. Bakers are artistic professionals who use frosting as their medium, and they often have brilliant ideas.

A wedding cake can be made to match the design of the wedding, the personality of the bride and groom, the wedding flowers, or even the pattern or style of a wedding gown. If you are having a destination wedding, the cake might be designed to resemble the venue or location. Options for cake shape and decoration are limitless; you can go with a traditional look or opt for something truly unique. Here are a few important things to consider:

FLAVOR: If you have trouble deciding on a single cake or filling flavor, request a cake with multiple tiers, and choose a different flavor for each tier. Once the cake is sliced and plated, guests can pick their favorites (or try them all!).

FILLINGS: The possibilities for cake fillings are almost endless. Some bakers have specialties, so ask what has been a hit with their previous clients. You can personalize your cake by choosing a fruit filling that alludes to your origins or background, or you can opt for a flavor that recalls the dessert you shared on your first date. Just be sure to sample your filling selections along with their corresponding cake flavors. Chocolate cake with lemon filling may not be the best combination!

FONDANT AND FROSTING: When it comes to decorating the exterior of your cake, there are two primary options—fondant and buttercream frosting. Fondant is sugar dough that the baker rolls out into a thin sheet and molds to the outside of the cake. It looks smooth and uniform, but can be lacking in the taste department. Buttercream cannot be shaped as easily as fondant, and it lacks fondant's immaculate appearance, but it tastes delicious. However, since buttercream is more susceptible to heat and the elements, a buttercream cake needs to be frosted and eaten within a shorter period of time.

FLOWERS: Frosting or sugar flowers can be beautiful and delicious, but they can also be expensive. If you are concerned about your budget, real flowers might be the way to go. Just make sure to coordinate with your baker and your florist. The flowers for your cake should be of an appropriate size and weight, and the cake should be able to support them. You can also add flowers around the bottom of your cake. This serves the double purpose of masking the stand or base of the cake and polishing the total presentation.

father on the dance floor, and they swayed to "Thank Heaven for Little Girls." With a tear in his eye, John hugged his daughter and announced that he had one last surprise for the happy couple. At that moment, Jane and Matthew were presented with a magnificent wedding cake. The elaborate confection was tall, white, and covered in pink roses and white flowers sculpted in icing. Scrollwork done in icing and faux diamond embellishments made each tier look intricate and glamorous. The design of the cake fit perfectly with the décor of both the ceremony and the reception, and it brought the night to a sweet conclusion.

After dessert, the bridal couple and their guests danced to jazz standards and favorite oldies. When the evening came to a close, the attendees were treated to one last surprise: a hand-blown glass flower was given to each guest as a memento of the evening. Each flower was wrapped in a white box tied with a pink ribbon. The favors were accompanied by farewell notes from the bride and groom, thanking their friends and family for attending.

Before departing with her new husband, Jane took a moment to express her gratitude toward her father with a heartfelt toast. He had given her a wedding that was far beyond anything she could have daydreamed, and John delighted in the knowledge that he had given his little girl a celebration that she would never forget.

TUTERA TIP:
For a truly individualized dessert experience, order a vanilla cake with vanilla frosting, and set up a toppings station. Allow your guests to choose from a vast array of fillings, sauces, and other tasty trimmings.

OVERVIEW:

FASHION:

The bride wore a strapless mermaid-cut gown made of white satin with a beaded neckline and a chapel-length veil. Her bridesmaids wore cappuccino-colored floor-length gowns.

INVITATION:

White panel cards were printed in silver script and embellished with faux diamonds.

COLOR SWATCHES/ FLORAL GUIDE

COLORS: white, pink, silver

FLOWERS: white, pink, and cream-colored roses; pink and white carnations; white stephanotis; white calla lilies; white phalaenopsis orchids

Specialty Drink:
Sweet Strawberry Splash

1 ½ oz. vodka

½ oz. strawberry liqueur

Splash of pink Prosecco

Fresh strawberries

Combine the vodka and strawberry liqueur in a
martini shaker with ice. Shake and strain into a
martini glass, top with Prosecco, and garnish with a
strawberry.

Menu:

FIRST COURSE

Jumbo lump crabmeat with tarragon
and avocado

Red and yellow tomato carpaccio with
rainbow greens and balsamic glaze

ENTRÉE

Miso-glazed sea bass with frizzled
leeks and a soy-and-wine reduction
on a bed of wasabi potatoes, grilled
asparagus, and baby carrots

Aged Black Angus New York strip
steak with blue cheese polenta,
spinach, and Cabernet sauce

DESSERT

Trio of sorbets (coconut, raspberry,
and mango)

Fresh berries, chocolate almond
praline tulip, raspberry coulis

Vanilla pear with pear sorbet and
caramel sauce

Wedding cake

MUSIC SUGGESTIONS:

FIRST DANCE

"Fly With Me"
– Kari Kimmel, from *Tinker Bell*

"I Could Not Ask for More"
– Edwin McCain

FATHER-DAUGHTER DANCE

"Let Your Heart Sing"
– Katharine McPhee, from *Tinker Bell*

"Thank Heaven for Little Girls"
– Maurice Chevalier

MOTHER-SON DANCE

"Your Mother and Mine"
– from *Peter Pan*

"I'll Stand by You" – the Pretenders

FAVOR:

Jane and Matthew's guests took home the
personalized crystal paperweights that served
as their place cards, in addition to hand-blown
glass flowers.

DISNEY TOUCHES:
Peter Pan / Tinker Bell

✿ Lighting is important at any wedding, but it was especially important for Jane and Matthew's indoor celebration. The soft pink glow of their reception area was enhanced by gobo lights that projected floral shapes throughout the space. For a Tinker Bell-inspired wedding, have the walls of your reception room lit with soft lavender light and request gobos shaped like starry swirls of pixie dust. You'll feel as though you're in Never Land!

✿ A good marriage requires faith, trust, and a little bit of pixie dust! Jane's bouquet was lightly dusted with sparkling glitter that gave her flowers a special shimmer. Floral "fairy dust" can be recommended by any florist, or found in a craft store and applied with a paintbrush to the petals of your bouquet flowers.

✿ Flowers are more important for some brides than they are for others, and John wanted Jane's wedding to look like a blooming fairy garden. Since Jane loved pink roses and white phalaenopsis orchids, both were featured prominently in the design of her wedding. If you'd like your centerpieces to look as though they've come from Pixie Hollow, choose your favorite flowers, and place glittery votive candleholders around the base of each arrangement.

✿ If you're looking for a wedding cake that's fabulous both inside and out, take your time choosing a baker, and consult with him or her about decorating options. Jane and Matthew's cake sparkled with faux diamonds, but you can achieve a subtler glimmer by having your baker use edible luster dust—it will seem as though the icing were whipped up by Tink herself! You may also want to ask your baker if he/she can construct sugar fairies out of fondant or pipe fairies onto the cake with royal icing. The sky is the limit!

✿ Your wedding favor should be a reflection of something you enjoy, and fairies enjoy nothing more than helping things grow! Jane and Matthew gave their guests glass flowers to take home, but if you're looking for a less expensive option, consider giving your guests flower seeds. As your friends and family watch their flowers grow, they'll think of you and the fun they had at your wedding!

CHAPTER FIVE

A Beach Dream Wedding

ON A STARLIT SUMMER NIGHT in Florida, two strangers met at a beach lounge party hosted by a group of mutual friends. Luz and Tim spent the entire night talking, and when the sun began to rise the next morning, the two were still sitting on the sand, deep in conversation about everything from modern art to their favorite dance clubs. Luz and Tim found that they had much more in common than a mutual friend; they were both New Yorkers with an affinity for good restaurants, city nightlife, traveling the globe, and, of course, the ocean. By the time they left Florida, they had embarked on a new relationship that would grow into lasting love.

The two had busy New York City lives—one was a corporate lawyer and the other was a publicist—but they always made time to steal away to a beach every now and then for a romantic vacation. The beach played a key role in Luz and Tim's relationship; they both were enchanted by the water, and their favorite moments together were spent on sun-kissed islands surrounded by turquoise seas. In honor of their five-year anniversary as a couple, Tim

took Luz on a spontaneous getaway to an island off Key West. He proposed on the beach in the state where they had met, and, needless to say, Luz said "yes."

When we met the engaged couple, Luz told us that the beach was where they felt "contentment that could last forever." This sounded like a great foundation for a marriage, and it was easy to see why they dreamed of celebrating their love with their family and

*D*estination Weddings

WHEN PLANNING A DESTINATION WEDDING, always be mindful of how comfortable your guests will be. Select a destination where the temperature is comfortable and provide invitees with information about the altitude, climate, and recommended clothing. Check out the seasonal weather patterns for the destination you choose. For tropical destinations, be wary of hurricane season and the hottest months of the year; you don't want your guests to be caught up in a storm or stuck in an airport. If the ceremony is taking place outside near the water, look up a tide schedule and choose a day when high tide will coincide with the time of your wedding. Beaches at low tide sometimes smell like silt and are often cluttered with seaweed.

Make it as easy as possible for your guests to check "yes" on their RSVP cards. Consider a time when the majority of your friends and family will be able to travel. Consult with a travel agent and select a destination that allows for flexibility with regards to airlines and flight times. Offer multiple hotel and accommodation choices that vary in price. Choose a host hotel that will serve as a hub (and where you, yourselves, will stay) and look into group rates. Also keep in mind that the more remote your location, the more expensive it will be to import food, flowers, and any other elements you'll need. Shipping over long distances also takes up time and requires extra planning for punctual deliveries.

friends by the sea. Naturally, a couple so inclined toward all things oceanic immediately put us in mind of Ariel and Prince Eric from *The Little Mermaid*. Like Ariel, Luz was spirited, adventurous, and wholeheartedly devoted to her prince. After she had recounted the story of their relationship, we all agreed that it would only be right to continue their Floridian tradition and hold their wedding in the Sunshine State.

Gathering friends and family together in a fantastic locale sets an exciting tone for a wedding right from the start. Luz and Tim planned to host one hundred and fifty guests at their gathering, and these guests would be coming from all over the world; Luz's entire family would be traveling from Brazil. Florida was a perfect choice because it held special meaning for Luz and Tim, and it was also easily accessible for their guests. We encourage couples to choose destinations that are both guest-accessible and able to provide the resources needed to host an event. Remote islands are romantic, but choosing them can lead to complications when you're trying to plan a wedding! It was a priority for this couple to have as many of their favorite people—who lived in scattered locations from São Paulo to Seattle—share in their joys on the beach. So, choosing a location that would encourage their guests to attend was critical.

When he proposed to Luz, Tim had told her that if she asked, he would "give her the world." We joked that she did indeed ask—but it was *Disney* World that she requested. Since a good portion of her family was unfamiliar with the States—and also excited to see the country's sites—Luz wanted them to experience the joys of one of her favorite destinations: Walt Disney World. After coming such a long way, her guests would be able to

see Luz get married, and enjoy a vacation in the place where magic makes dreams come true. And perhaps most importantly, Disney World would provide Luz with the opportunity to enjoy the reception of a lifetime.

As much as she loved the breezy beach, Luz still wanted her wedding to be structured and formal. An oceanfront ceremony combined with a black-tie reception at Disney World was the perfect solution. She considered the choices available in the Couture Wedding Collection by David Tutera that we had designed exclusively for Disney's Fairy Tale Weddings, and she selected the "Simply Chic" option. This allowed her to relinquish the duties of planning the celebration logistics and hand the reins over to the Disney professionals. Having a team plan the reception left more time for Luz and Tim to have fun with their guests during the days leading up to the wedding.

TUTERA TIP:
For a beach wedding, send a message in a bottle in lieu of an invitation. Handwrite the pertinent information in black ink on ivory paper, roll it into a tube, and tie it with a piece of twine. Funnel the scrolled invitation into an empty, clear bottle, and add small seashells, crystals, sand, and pearls. Cork or screw the top back on and package it securely before sending it to a guest.

The next important step in the planning process was choosing a location for the ceremony. We took the bride and groom on a tour through the east coast of Florida, looking for a beach that would be romantic, beautiful, and easily accessible. As we traveled, Luz and Tim picked up postcards featuring beautiful Florida beaches, and wrote a note to each of their guests. These postcards served as their Save the Dates. Each one proclaimed: "Having a great time! Wish you were here—Hope you will join us for a beach wedding on June, 29, 2008! Love, Luz and Tim."

After combing many different sandy strands, the bridal couple settled upon a beach estate in Melbourne. While growing up, Tim had spent his summers there at his grandparent's beachfront Victorian-inspired home. It was important to the groom that he be able to exchange vows with his bride on the beach where he had played with his cousins as a child.

Once the ceremony location was finalized, it was time to begin visualizing the design of the reception. Luz and Tim wanted a wedding that was similar to their relationship. They had fantastic, modern taste and loved going to parties. But the easygoing pair also enjoyed traveling, relaxing, and spending time with their families. Luz—fun, friendly, and appreciative of life—found beauty in simplicity, and she wanted her reception to be classy and elegant as opposed to over the top.

Since Luz and Tim had experienced their two most romantic moments in Florida (their

first meeting and Tim's proposal), we thought it only appropriate to re-create these elements for their wedding. The beachside ceremony would be reminiscent of the proposal, while the reception would be lounge-like, and throughout it all, we would weave in a bit of sophisticated New York formality. Overall, it would be very clean, chic, and fresh, with a natural color scheme featuring white, sandy beige, silver, and celadon green.

The invitations were the first medium upon which Luz and Tim could express the theme of their wedding. They wanted to establish a tone that married a fun beach ceremony with a black-tie lounge reception. This required a very stylish and non-traditional invitation. Clear Lucite rectangles with rounded corners were printed in a modern black font. The cards invited guests to join Luz and Tim for a beach wedding ceremony on the sands of Melbourne, with a chic wedding reception at the Grand Floridian Hotel in Disney World to follow. Accommodation cards were sent along with the invitations, suggesting that the guests choose a hotel on Disney World property to be near the reception. Itineraries were also included, explaining that transportation would be provided to the beach on the day of the ceremony, and likewise for the return trip to the Grand Floridian. A brunch was scheduled for the following day, and it was recommended that the guests continue their stays in the park to enjoy everything Disney World had to offer.

Finally, the day of the wedding arrived. Guests entering their rooms at various Walt Disney World resorts were treated to an arrival gift bag from Luz and Tim that was waiting on their beds. Woven straw beach bags had been filled with tropical treats, including travel-sized suntan lotions, leis, flip-flops, bottles of water with monogrammed labels, dried pineapple, and a welcome note tied to a box of Disney chocolates. We also added an assortment of brochures and tourist information pamphlets about Orlando and Disney park attractions, with suggestions of activities for guests to enjoy in their free time. A personalized map with pinpoints marking Luz and Tim's favorite rides, restaurants, and points of interest gave guests insight into the couple's love for Disney World. Lastly, an itinerary featuring the couple's monogram and printed in their wedding colors was tucked into each bag so that guests would be informed about every wedding event.

After a luxurious day spent getting ready in the Grand Floridian spa, Luz and her bridesmaids got into a limousine bound for the ceremony location, while the groom and his groomsmen rode in another limo. Shuttles picked up all the guests from their hotels and took them to Melbourne Beach. Once there, the wedding party and their guests encountered an oceanic wedding paradise.

TUTERA TIP:
Don't over-plan or under-plan your guests' time. Have activities available, but also give them downtime to explore the destination on their own.

TUTERA TIP:
Create a specialty cocktail, and give it a name that alludes to something about your relationship: your names, the place you met, or an interest you share. You could even have two: one for the groom and one for the bride! Display menus introducing the drink at the bar, and ask your cocktail waiters to explain its origin as they pass trays among your guests.

At the edge of the beach, a wooden platform had been erected and covered in sand-hued carpeting so that it blended perfectly with the shoreline. This allowed guests to feel as if they were sitting on the beach without actually getting their shoes sandy, and enabled us to hold a black-tie formal event in a beautiful, natural setting. Close to the softly crashing waves, one-hundred fifty natural wooden Chiavari chairs with white cushions had been set up for Luz and Tim's guests. On each chair lay a woven straw fan, its handle wrapped in thin green satin ribbon. Long strands of beach grass with pearls threaded onto them were glued to the fan, as were small shells, pearls, and white and green sea glass. While the guests awaited Luz's arrival, two butlers dressed in black tuxedos offered monogrammed bottles of water from silver trays.

Along each side of the aisle, sand-colored stone pedestals supported urns containing spherical flower arrangements made of large green hydrangea and jade roses. Three different types of candles gave dimension and structure

to the ceremony space; glass hurricanes shielding white tapers were set on oversized silver stands, silver-trimmed glass lanterns were positioned with white pillar candles inside, and tall cylindrical glass hurricanes holding more pillar candles were set on the ground. The use of glass containers served both practical and aesthetic purposes; they shielded the candles from beach wind and also introduced a clean glass element that was decidedly lighthouse-like.

A second ceremony platform was built to hold the bride and groom, the officiant, the bridal party, and the musicians. Weather forecasts told us that there would be a light breeze right before sunset, so we decided to use the ocean winds to our advantage to create a wistful, carefree scene. The platform was surrounded by bamboo poles supporting flowing white fabric banners that floated in

IF YOU ARE HAVING A SUMMERTIME BEACH WEDDING, keep your guests hydrated and cool by providing them with bottles of water and fans aplenty. If your celebration is taking place close to the water, make sure to have microphones for the ceremony. The sound of the waves may muffle your voices, so test the sound system beforehand to make sure your loved ones hear your vows! For a fun, casual summer wedding, provide flip-flops or alternative footwear options for your guests—especially if they will be standing in the sand. You might want to consider having your service at sunset. Mother Nature will paint a glorious picture of color behind you! Research the anticipated sunset time, locate the best spot, and don't be late! You want your guests to be able to see you and your wedding party under the orange-pink glow of the sky! Ideally, your ceremony should begin thirty to forty-five minutes prior to sunset time.

the breeze. To ensure that the wind didn't blow away anything that was meant to stay put, we anchored down the décor, ceremony programs, and other loose items with shells, starfish, and clear glass containers holding white pillar candles. The natural simplicity of the ceremony was inspiring; the ocean waves and blue sky were nature's beautiful backdrop.

The bridesmaids wore light and breezy tea-length halter dresses made of pale blue chiffon, and paired them with matching high heel sandals. The look was simultaneously fit for the beach and formal enough for a black-tie affair. As the bridesmaids walked down the aisle, they carried bouquets of white tulips accented with green leaves. The stems of each bouquet were wrapped in a white satin ribbon, and a generous bow was tied at the base of the blooms.

TUTERA TIP:
Destination weddings can disrupt your circadian rhythm if they take place in a different time zone. Dodge the drowsiness of jet lag and plan to arrive at least one day ahead of time so that you can get acclimated to the location. Advise your guests to do the same!

Luz's gown was a long sheath of airy white chiffon that created a graceful silhouette. She carried a bouquet of white tulips, green parrot tulips, lily grass, white dendrobians, green anthurium, lily of the valley, and calla lilies. Tim wore a stylish matching boutonniere made with white tulips and lily grass in a seashell. In an intimate ceremony, the couple poured two colors of sand into one bottle to signify their union, and Luz's sister read a passage called "Footprints in the Sand."

After the ceremony, guests were led to a cocktail area, just steps away. We had created a tropical lounge where lights were strung from thatched palapas underneath a canopy of palm trees. Rattan chairs and white cushions and pillows surrounded wooden tables, and white pillar candles glowed as the sun began to set. A strolling guitarist played as linen-clad waiters served three specialty cocktails.

Before the sky turned dark, the guests departed the cocktail reception. At the edge of the sand, a tuxedoed "shoe butler" dusted sand off guests' shoes before they boarded the shuttles. Once the shuttles were en route, monitors dropped down from their ceilings and displayed a montage of photos and video footage of the bride and groom growing up. The movie made the hour-long ride back to Disney World fly by, and before they knew it, the guests were debarking at the Grand Floridian Resort.

Luz and Tim's reception took place in the resort's grand ballroom. In order to transform the ballroom into a sleek and trendy atmosphere, we had draped every wall in white fabric and suspended white spherical lanterns of varying sizes from the ceiling. Tall rectangular mirrors in thick silver frames were propped against two walls, and little ledges on each mirror held votive candles whose flames were reflected in the glass. The tables were draped in a sheer white cloth with payettes (large sequin-like discs) and silver Chiavari chairs with matching chair covers were placed at each table.

We like to use clear and reflective surfaces like glass and Lucite to create illusion and shape in a space. These types of material create a sophisticated, modern environment without being heavy on the eye. For Luz and Tim's wedding, Lucite towers gave the reception a clean look with a bit of an edge. Some of the tables featured rectangular Lucite towers

reflective surfaces were filled with orchids, hydrangea, and calla lilies.

Lastly, for Luz and Tim's two long tables, we made elaborate centerpiece arrangements out of white calla lilies accented with orchids. The stems of the lilies were tied at the middle and the blooms were positioned to face both upward and downward. For a very distinctive appearance, the calla lily heads that faced downward were submerged underwater in clear containers.

topped with square votives. Inside these towers, vases contained white calla lilies of varying stem lengths resting on a pave of white rose blossoms. Some towers had embedded ledges that held orchids. To add dimension to the tables, we also placed clear vases upside down and suspended orchid heads inside them. Our favorite tables had runners comprised of long, low Lucite containers that held short white pillar candles on glass candle stands. Green orchids hung from each candle, and the runners were filled with more green orchids, white rose petals, and white gerbera daisies. Other containers with hard edges or

To create a chic, lounge-like atmosphere and to draw attention to the location of the food and beverages, we chose to use illuminated white cocktail bars. On top of the bars we placed several bouquets in clear cylindrical vases. Each arrangement was comprised of one type of flower: Casablanca lilies, green hydrangea, white roses, or jade roses. The stems were cut short and wrapped in green leaves for a clean, fresh look.

The prominent use of white gave the room a modern, sophisticated quality, but we wanted to add dimension to the décor. In order to create texture and visual interest, we made sure to incorporate intricate details into every aspect of the design. White china was set out on white tables, but the square tables were set with round plates and the round tables were set with square plates. On each place setting, a white napkin was accompanied by a green orchid head. The silver flatware was smooth and sleek, and the conical glassware furthered the martini lounge concept.

After dinner, the illuminated cocktail bars were converted into dessert bars. Luz and Tim had both confessed to having a sweet tooth, and they wanted their dessert course to feature all of their favorites. Tiered Lucite dessert trays held cones of cotton candy, rows of chocolate truffles dusted with powdered sugar and cocoa, sugared doughnuts, chocolate-dipped coconut bites, dark chocolate éclairs, cupcakes, and candied apples. The grand finale of the dessert course was a four-tiered wedding cake that was displayed on top of a Lucite box containing square votive candles. The cake had been created to match the look of the party, and it was constructed with both square and round layers covered in pale green and white fondant. But in order to give the confection a bit of a fun, funky edge, several patterns and decorative elements were deliberately mismatched and combined. Pearls, crystals, lace, diamond jacquard print, vertical stripes, and scalloped edges created a whimsical look that was finished off with clusters of fresh green orchids.

Following the cake cutting, the party transformed into a nightclub. The dance floor was lit with swirling, colored lights and soon it was filled with guests moving to the beats played by an energetic deejay.

Near midnight Tim asked his bride and their families to join him outside on the Grand Floridian beach. He had arranged for a boat to take him and his bride on a moonlit sail so that they could enjoy a private moment together before settling in for the night.

After Tim and Luz sailed away, their guests were delighted to find a table covered in sand and shells that displayed the couple's wedding favors. Green and white leather luggage tags held notes that read, "Thank you for sharing our special day!" The next day, the newly married couple spent time with their guests in the "happiest place on earth" celebrating what had been the happiest day of their lives.

OVERVIEW:

FASHION:

The bride wore a long sheath gown made of airy white chiffon.

The bridesmaids wore tea-length halter dresses made of pale blue chiffon, and paired them with matching high heel sandals.

INVITATION:

Luz and Tim's invitations were Lucite rectangles with rounded edges printed in a modern black font.

COLOR SWATCHES/ FLORAL GUIDE

COLORS: shades of green, white, cream

FLOWERS: jade roses, white roses, green dendrobrium orchids, white calla lilies, green hydrangea

SPECIALTY DRINK: SEASCAPE BREEZE

1 ½ oz. vodka

¾ oz. peach schnapps

½ oz. creme de cassis

2 oz. cranberry juice

Orange slice for garnish

Maraschino cherry for garnish

Pour all the ingredients into a shaker with ice. Shake well and strain into a glass. Garnish with fruit.

MENU:

FIRST COURSE

Wasabi-seared scallops encrusted in lemon grass and sesame seeds served over a nitshiki rice cake with orange tobiko roe

Tat soi greens with Japanese chrysanthemums and a plum wine and soy vinaigrette

SECOND COURSE

Cantaloupe ginger sorbet

THIRD COURSE

Tsao-style prime beef filet

Sweet Thai chili butter braised grouper

Daikon radish, pureed potatoes, and petite Asian-style vegetables

FOURTH COURSE

Miniature desserts including cotton candy, chocolate truffles, sugared doughnuts, chocolate-dipped coconut bites, dark chocolate éclairs, cupcakes, and candied apples

Wedding cake

MUSIC SUGGESTIONS:

FIRST DANCE

"One Dance" – Jodi Benson
(Ariel from *The Little Mermaid*)

"At Last" – Etta James

FATHER-DAUGHTER DANCE

"Beautiful in My Eyes"
– Joshua Kadison

"Somewhere Over the Rainbow"
– Israel Kamakawiwi'ole

MOTHER-SON DANCE

"Sweet Child o' Mine" – Sheryl Crow

"Three Times a Lady"
– the Commodores

FAVOR:

For their destination wedding, Luz and Tim gave their guests white and green leather luggage tags. Inside each tag was a message that read, "Thank you for sharing our special day!"

DISNEY TOUCHES:
The Little Mermaid

❀ A destination wedding can be an adventure for you and your guests. Luz and Tim held their ceremony at a Florida beach so that they could be near the rolling waves. For a nautical wedding like Ariel and Eric's in *The Little Mermaid*, you could rent a yacht, charter a tall ship, or tie the knot on a cruise.

❀ The colors of your wedding help to set the tone of the celebration. We used primarily white, cream, and green to give Luz and Tim's wedding a fresh, seaside feeling. If you want your reception to seem like it's "Under the Sea," you could opt for shades of purple, blue, and green.

❀ If a majority of your guests are traveling from a considerable distance, welcoming gift baskets are a great way of thanking them for making the trip. And since Ariel is always collecting treasures, this is a wonderful way of incorporating a *Little Mermaid* theme. We filled straw beach bags with all sorts of tropical goodies, but you might want to have custom totes embroidered with your monogram. Fill them with seashell-shaped soaps, bath salts, saltwater taffy, and maybe even a *dinglehopper* or a *snarfblat*!

❀ Your centerpieces are strong focal points at your reception, so make sure that they tie into your design concept. We made several different kinds of centerpieces for Luz and Tim's wedding but they were tied together with common elements like Lucite and calla lilies. For a reception that looks like the halls of Atlantica, create centerpieces that look like coral and adorn them with strings of pearls, shells, and sea glass.

❀ Beach-themed wedding cakes can be fun, formal, or a combination of both. Luz and Tim's cake was decorated in green and white and was embellished with pearls and crystals. If you'd like a cake fit for Triton's daughter, ask your baker to make scallop shells out of white chocolate and use them as accents on your cake.

CHAPTER SIX

A Country Dream Wedding

SOMETIMES, the most magical moments occur when you take a step back and appreciate everything that you might otherwise take for granted. Many weddings are about creating a brand-new experience—something never before seen. But for some couples, a meaningful wedding day is spent in familiar surroundings, as they enjoy renewed appreciation for cherished places, family, and friends.

Jennifer had grown up in a quaint country town in Pennsylvania. Some might say that her hometown seemed to be plucked out of another place and time, a calm and peaceful setting where all of the neighbors were friendly, clothes were hung out in the sun to dry, and rocking chairs swayed lazily on every front porch. It was a close-knit farming community, the members of which frequently gathered together to celebrate accomplishments, holidays, and important milestones. So it was no wonder that Jennifer had never felt the inclination to leave—she was happy teaching horseback riding, gardening, and taking long walks with her dogs.

Michael, on the other hand, was born and raised in Pittsburgh. He had stayed in the city through college, and gotten a job in real estate development. Driven and ambitious, he was excited when his boss sent him to research a potential project in Jennifer's town. He hoped that—if successful—it might lead to a promotion. But Michael had no idea that it would lead to love.

Michael told us that after inspecting a proposed site for a horse farm, he decided to take advantage of the sunny afternoon and explore the wooded trails around the property. But after an hour of wandering, he was thoroughly lost. He remembered that he had just closed his cell phone—which had no reception—when a dog trotted over and dropped a tennis ball at his feet. Moments later, Jennifer appeared. An avid hiker, she knew the trails well and agreed to show him the way back to his car. Before long, Michael's trips out to the country became a regular occurrence, and as he fell in love with Jennifer, he fell in love with her town as well. After he proposed, they bought a small farm, moved in together, and began planning their dream wedding.

When we arrived in Pennsylvania, we immediately understood why Michael and Jennifer were so in love with country living. The open fields and wooded areas were a pleasant departure from busy, over-developed cities and buzzing metropolises. It was a welcome respite for us to be planning a celebration that would embody the warmth of country hospitality. We set out to create a delightful down-home wedding in a sweetly provincial town that was as charming as the bride and groom.

In the area where the couple lived, there was little more than a general store, a few specialty shops, and the church that Jennifer and Michael attended every Sunday to hear Jennifer's uncle give the sermon. Jennifer's uncle would be performing their marriage ceremony in that very same church. After the ceremony, the couple would proceed down a winding two-lane road to a hundred-year-old barn. Restored and refurbished to look as it did when it was first built, the barn would serve as the venue for Jennifer and Michael's wedding reception.

The bridal couple wanted an autumn wedding with an old-fashioned ceremony, followed by a more modern "country chic" celebration—a mix of old and new. Jennifer spent a lot of time volunteering for a non-profit organization that specialized in helping businesses "go green," so it was important to her that her wedding be as environmentally friendly as possible. When she told us that she also rode horses, grew her own vegetables, and loved to go on kayaking trips—and that Michael was a city boy who worked for a big real estate company—we thought, "She's a modern-day Pocahontas who has met her John Smith!"

The natural beauty of their surroundings inspired us to choose a color palette of

soothing earth tones for their wedding. And the rustic, yet elegant atmosphere of the barn called to mind Victorian brocade fabrics, antique laces, velvets, and satins. The reception would have an underlying tone of old-world richness with a hint of contemporary flair—a perfect fit for Michael and Jennifer.

To give their friends and family a hint of what their wedding would be like, Jennifer and Michael selected invitations that were both organic-looking and elegant. For each invitation, a piece of cream-colored paper was centered on a slightly larger piece of brown card stock and printed with a subtle lace pattern. A band of antique lace was wrapped around each card and secured with a monogrammed paper "brooch."

When it came to designing the ceremony space, we wanted to accent the beauty of the environment without overshadowing it. The idyllic one-room church sat on a meadow surrounded by a white-picket fence, brick walkways, and colorful flower beds, and we wanted the interior of the church to look just as picturesque as the outside. To frame the aisle, silver candle stands holding short white tapers were positioned at intervals along each side. Floral garlands were wrapped around each of these, giving them a soft, natural look, and baskets of white and pale pink roses were hung from the ends of the pews with white satin bows. Arrangements of roses, white hydrangeas, and flowering dogwood branches were placed on top of the altar, the pulpit, and the organ to bring the beauty of the outdoors inside.

On a beautiful day in September, Jennifer and Michael's guests arrived at her uncle's church for an afternoon service. After everyone had taken their seats, the organist began to play Pachelbel's "Canon in D Major." Three bridesmaids walked down the aisle wearing lacy cream-colored, tea-length dresses and elegant shawls. Each bridesmaid carried a very unique bouquet: three different antique purses had been filled with three very different flower arrangements. The blooms were a mixture of pink and white roses, green and purple hydrangeas, white helleboris, lilacs, lisianthus, and ivy foliage. When the last bridesmaid had joined Michael at the altar, Jennifer appeared at the head of the aisle.

Jennifer's bouquet was an arrangement of white and pale pink roses, white peonies, white anemonies, basil, and sage. The bouquet handle was wrapped with antique Battenberg lace for a classy and delicate look. But what made Jennifer's bouquet truly special was the cameo brooch that was pinned to the lace. The brooch had been passed down through the generations by the women in Jennifer's family, and her mother had given it to her that very morning. When the bride began her journey down the aisle, the organ music ceased, and guests stood as a children's choir sang "Simple Gifts." Throughout the ceremony, the congregation sang a series of hymns that

Jennifer and Michael had chosen. Then the couple lit a unity candle, and Jennifer's uncle gave a very touching sermon about love and the new life that his niece was about to embark upon with her groom.

At the end of their wedding, Jennifer and Michael made sure to host a receiving line. With a guest list on the smaller side, it was appropriate for them to greet every attendee as he or she exited the church. It was also very fitting for the style of the wedding and for the couple; Jennifer and Michael wanted the opportunity to show their graciousness as hosts before heading to their reception party, where the pace would change and the fun would begin.

Wedding Bouquets

ADDING SPECIAL TOUCHES AND TWISTS to bridesmaid bouquets can bring energy and variety to a wedding ceremony. In Jennifer and Matthew's wedding, every girl wore the same dress, but each carried her own special bouquet. Jennifer actually picked the bouquets for each bridesmaid based on her personality. This is exactly the kind of gesture that can make each member of the bridal party feel special and included, and it adds a hint of surprise to the usual parade of matching dresses and flowers.

TUTERA TIP:
Personalize your bridal bouquet. Ask your florist to incorporate an heirloom piece of jewelry, or to wrap the handle of the bouquets in fabric taken from a meaningful garment— perhaps your mother or grandmother's wedding gown.

Fashion by Kirstie Kelly

FORGET TRACTOR PULLS AND HOEDOWNS—today's country weddings ooze sophistication and romanticism. Set against mother earth's exquisite backdrop, a country wedding is all about softness and playfulness, from the décor to the bridal gown and everything in between. Forget heavy satins and cathedral trains at country barn weddings, and remember airy fabrics and chapel length trains that float down the aisle.

Picture ball gowns in organza, lace, English tulle, and taffeta; or A-line dresses, sheaths, and fit and flare gowns in the lightest of fabrics. In looking for the ideal material, consider that country weddings are typically candle lit and opt for a fabric that will absorb the light rather than appear dull. In the same vein, select colors that will intermingle with the flickering candles to achieve warm hues.

In this wedding, texture was key. More specifically, lace—which beautifully harmonized with the country theme—was an elegant and distinctly feminine choice. With country barn weddings, brides walk the line between organically ethereal and fantastically formal with fabric selection as well as the intricacy of detail. For instance, a sparkling brooch or a sassy sash can catapult a bridal gown from understated to downright grand.

Jennifer chose to wear a sophisticated V-neck ball gown from the Disney Bridal Belle collection. The enchanting lace and organza gown featured a dropped waist and lace detail on the skirt, which harmonized with the bride's bouquet and the wedding invitations. A peach-colored sash secured with a flower-shaped crystal brooch fit perfectly with the décor of the reception and lent a touch of old world elegance to the ensemble. The bridesmaids' gowns were shorter, ivory-colored versions of the bride's gown, which gave the bridal party a unified, classy appearance.

Surrounded by rolling greens, blossoming flowers, and rustic settings, countryside weddings are far from down home, but rather showcase simplicity at its finest and, dare we say, most fairy tale-like.

The barn that Michael and Jennifer chose for their reception was a perfect fit for the tone of their wedding. All the history and charm of the building made the celebration authentic and genuine—a true extension of the couple's personalities. There was nothing elaborately manufactured or artificial to detract from the beauty of the natural setting. Through an arbor abounding with flowers and vines, the guests walked up a stone pathway to the entrance of the barn. Once inside, they encountered a refreshment table holding two silver drink dispensers—one contained lime ice water, and the other held rosemary-infused lemon water. When all had arrived, waiters led

Receiving Lines

RECEIVING LINES ARE A FORMAL, TRADITIONAL WAY to thank your guests for their presence; they also give guests the opportunity to offer their congratulations to the newlyweds. If you decide to have a receiving line, you can estimate that it will take thirty minutes to greet 100 guests. We always say that it's ideal to start your marriage together with greetings! The customary order of a receiving line is as follows:

BRIDE

GROOM

MOTHER OF THE BRIDE

FATHER OF THE BRIDE

MOTHER OF THE GROOM

FATHER OF THE GROOM

The host family (i.e., the ones who are paying for the majority of the wedding) line up first after the bride and groom. You may opt to keep it simple and limit the receiving line to these six people. But if you choose to continue on, the next in line would be the maid of honor and the best man. Plenty of couples stop here, but if you have the time—and the space!—you can also include the bridesmaids and the groomsmen.

When greeting your guests, always make eye contact! Keep things very sincere and short, so you're not spending too much time with any one person, and always keep people moving along to avoid having anyone wait too long. Once your guests have walked through the receiving line, you and your groom should exit in style! Plan ahead, so that your guests can blow bubbles, toss birdseed, or throw flower petals—as Jennifer and Matthew's guests did for their nature-inspired wedding.

On the wall nearest the entrance to the cocktail area, we had hung an empty wooden picture frame and pinned escort cards inside it with golden-pearl-headed pins. The bridesmaids hung their bouquets on nails underneath the frame, and then took the lead in finding their escort cards. The rest of the guests followed suit, and everyone went downstairs to the dinner reception.

For the décor of the main room, we took an eclectic approach that made the atmosphere seem redolent of an antiques shop. By layering and combining colors, textures, and materials, we were able to give the round tables a sophisticated look with plenty of fascinating details. Vintage

the guests up a wooden staircase. Clusters of candles of varying heights had been placed on each step to light the way with a welcoming glow. At the top, the guests entered a loft where cocktails were waiting to be sipped. One specialty drink was a rum-based country iced tea that was served in glass mason jars with floating lemon slices. The other sweet concoction, called Apple Blossom, was served with floating apple slices and mint leaves.

upholstered chairs were placed around the tables, which were draped with sheer linens featuring stripes and an embroidered vine design. Some of the tables were set with multi-armed silver candelabra, each of which held twenty glitter-coated honeycomb beeswax candles in a variety of colors. Other tables were decorated with a large quantity of pillar candles in multiple widths and heights—some measuring over eighteen inches tall, some over fourteen inches in diameter. The predominant colors of both designs were cream, sage, burgundy, and rose, which harmonized perfectly with the natural setting.

Amid the glowing candles were flower arrangements and antique curiosities—ranging from vintage milk bottles to silver bird figurines—that were deliberately mismatched, making each table setting unique. On one table, a small hammered-silver vase held a cluster of pink roses; on another, a glass bowl overflowed with purple lisianthus. Brown dupioni silk napkins were folded and bound with strips of antique lace, and each lace "napkin ring" was accented with a unique heirloom or brooch. Two different types of glassware were chosen to add further variety, insuring that no two tables would look exactly alike.

TUTERA TIP:
Instead of using regular filler greens in your bouquets and arrangements, use the herbs right out of your garden! Basil, lavender, and sage all make beautiful (and beautifully scented) fillers!

Aside from the napkins and table linens, the other unifying elements were the charger plates and flatware. The white china charger plates were perfectly suited to the old-fashioned theme, with intricate rims that resembled white lace. Antiqued silver flatware looked as if it had been pulled right out of Grandmother's cupboards.

When it came time to eat, Jennifer and Michael's guests were treated to a medley of delicious comfort foods. Truffle macaroni and cheese, filet mignon encrusted with espresso grounds, and citrus pumpkin pie with Grand Marnier cream were all modernized courses of an upscale yet familiar dinner for Jennifer, Michael, and their friends and family.

With so much to interest the eye on each table, we left the barn walls and floor undecorated, so that guests could appreciate the building in its original splendor. Strands of lights on the rafters overhead gave the room a soft radiance—just like twilight on an autumn day. At one end of the barn, a deejay set up his speakers as four instrumentalists, including a guitarist player and a fiddle player, got ready to provide live entertainment.

After finishing dinner, the couple and their guests hit the dance floor. The deejay and the live musicians alternated sets so that the partygoers could groove to contemporary hits and also square-dance to familiar favorites. The country band had an infectious energy, and it wasn't long before guests were line-dancing and swinging their partners across the barn floor.

After a few rounds of the Virginia reel, the revelers gathered to watch Jennifer and Michael cut their wedding cake. Or should we say, "cakes"? For one last twist on a traditional wedding element, the bride and groom had chosen to have five smaller cakes of different sizes, shapes, colors, and styles. The cakes

coordinated flawlessly with the overall design of the wedding, and they looked beautiful; each one had a different element that made it stand out. All five cakes were covered in fondant, but the colors ranged from sage to violet, to echo the table décor. Each confection on its own was a work of artistry; one was covered with frosting pearls; another had lavender blooms made of sugar that resembled one of the bridesmaid's bouquets. In addition to their individual exteriors, the cakes were each flavored and filled with different ingredients. One cake was vanilla-flavored, with whipped cream and fresh strawberries (a nod to the bride's love of strawberry shortcake), one was devil's food cake with dark chocolate ganache, and another was carrot cake with cream-cheese filling. Guests delighted in sampling all the different flavors, and the cakes were the talk of the town long after the wedding had ended.

Jennifer and Michael put a great deal of thought into choosing the perfect favors for their wedding. They wanted to give their guests parting gifts that were tasteful, useful, and related to the style of their wedding. Since the couple shared a love of reading, they decided upon golden leaf-shaped bookmarks tied with golden tassels. The bookmarks looked as though they could have been part of the antique-inspired décor, and the leaf shape represented the bride and groom's love of the outdoors. And not only were the bookmarks beautiful—they were functional! Any time friends or family members used the bookmark, they would be reminded of the glorious autumn day that they spent celebrating Jennifer and Michael's marriage. As everyone departed for the evening, they knew that they had witnessed a union of two people with very different backgrounds who had been brought together by a love that was at once old-fashioned, new-fangled, and truly timeless.

Wedding Favors

YOUR WEDDING FAVORS are the final sentence in your wedding story—your last chance to make a statement to your guests and thank them for helping you celebrate your marriage. The best favors aren't necessarily the most elaborate; they just need to be selected tastefully, presented properly, and coordinated with the overall style of your wedding. Personalize your favors by adding hints of your wedding colors, adding mementos from your venue, or incorporating your monogram. Here are a few of our favorite favor ideas:

Luggage tags

Candy apples

Fans

Crystal paperweights

Blankets or pashmina scarves

Bottles of wine with personalized labels

Chocolates

A family recipe printed on a card and attached to either the finished product or the necessary ingredients

Jars full of color-themed candy

Herbs in small, galvanized pots

Spiced-cider mix, hot-cocoa mix, or iced-tea mix

Jars of jam, hot fudge sauce, honey, salsa, barbecue sauce, or other condiments

Recipes and ingredients/tools to make your signature drink

Apples in a burlap bag with an apple pie recipe

CDs of music heard at the wedding

S'mores kits with marshmallow skewers

Seeds or flower bulbs

OVERVIEW:

FASHION:

The bride wore a V-neck ball gown from the Disney Bridal Belle collection. The gown was made of lace and organza, with a dropped waist and a peach-colored sash.

The bridesmaids wore ivory-colored tea-length dresses, also made of lace and organza and cut in the same style as the bride's gown.

INVITATION:

Jennifer and Michael's elegant invitations were made using cream-colored paper centered on pieces of brown card stock. They were printed with a subtle lace pattern, and a band of antique lace was wrapped around each card and secured with a monogrammed paper "brooch."

COLOR SWATCHES/ FLORAL GUIDE:

COLORS: burgundy, sage green, white, cream, pink, violet

FLOWERS: green and purple hydrangeas, lilacs, pink and white roses, ivy, purple lisianthus, white helleboris, muscari, lavender, champagne roses, fiddle fern, garden herbs

SPECIALTY DRINK: SWEETEST'S TEA

5 oz. iced tea

1 ¼ oz. spiced rum

½ tsp. lemon juice

Combine iced tea, rum, and lemon juice. Serve over ice in a mason jar.

MENU:

FIRST COURSE

Cucumber basket of field greens, teardrop tomatoes, toasted pine nuts, and sundried strawberries, with white balsamic vinaigrette

Macaroni and cheese with truffle oil

ENTRÉE

Rosemary lamb, lemon pepper shrimp, char-grilled chicken, or seared tuna, with red, yellow, and green peppers, red onions, and cherry tomatoes

Char-grilled Black Angus filet mignon encrusted with espresso grounds, with fingerling potatoes, broccoli rabe, and yellow squash

DESSERT

Citrus pumpkin pie with Grand Marnier cream

Classic warm apple torte with vanilla ice cream

Wedding cakes

MUSIC SUGGESTIONS:

FIRST DANCE

"If I Never Knew You" – Jon Secada and Shanice, from *Pocahontas*

"Have I Told You Lately" – Van Morrison

FATHER-DAUGHTER DANCE

"Colors of the Wind" – Vanessa Williams, from *Pocahontas*

"You've Got a Friend" – James Taylor

MOTHER-SON DANCE

"Forever Young" – Rod Stewart

"If I Could" – Barbra Streisand

FAVOR:

Jennifer and Michael gave their guests golden leaf-shaped bookmarks with golden tassels.

DISNEY TOUCHES: *Pocahontas*

✿ Choosing a location for the ceremony that has personal significance will make your wedding that much more meaningful. Jennifer and Michael were wed by her uncle in the church she had attended every Sunday since her childhood. If you and your groom feel a strong tie with nature, like Pocahontas and John Smith, get married outside! Research local parks and nature reserves and find one with a grove of willow trees. Hold your ceremony underneath the weeping branches, and you'll feel as if you have your very own Grandmother Willow.

✿ Jennifer's mother gave her a family heirloom—a cameo brooch—just before the ceremony, which Jennifer pinned to the lace on her bouquet handle. Pocahontas wouldn't have carried flowers at her wedding, but she most definitely would have worn her mother's necklace. If you have a piece of jewelry that means a lot to you, wear it!

✿ By no means do your wedding favors have to be expensive—but they should be thoughtful! The leaf-shaped bookmarks that Jennifer and Michael gave to their guests were functional, and cost-efficient, and they symbolized the couple's love of the outdoors. For a *Pocahontas*-inspired favor, you might choose to give your guests leather journals or silver compasses.

✿ The invitations that Jennifer and Michael sent to their friends and family were perfect precursors for a country wedding with an Old-World-meets-New-World theme. If you'd like to incorporate elements from *Pocahontas* into your invitations, consider selecting a design that features green hummingbirds like Flit, or tall ships like the one John Smith sailed to Virginia.

✿ Pocahontas and her tribe knew that it was important to respect the earth and protect the environment, and those priorities are more important now than ever before. Using vintage and antique materials cuts down on the need for unnecessary manufacturing, and using eco-friendly vendors reduces waste. Rent cloth napkins instead of buying paper ones, equip light fixtures with energy-efficient bulbs, and place recycling bins next to your bar for empty bottles and cans.

CHAPTER SEVEN

A Traditional Dream Wedding

SOME LITTLE GIRLS BEGIN DREAMING about their wedding day before they've even developed their first crushes, and Jenna was no different. After attending her first wedding at a young age, she was taken with everything about it: the flowers, the gowns, the tiaras . . . . Simply put, Jenna fell in love with weddings. She was enthralled with the idea of a chivalrous groom and a princess bride promising to love each other forever.

Always a hopeless romantic, Jenna grew into a kind and giving woman whose good-hearted approach to life was infectious and cherished by those around her. So it was no surprise to Jenna's family when her boyfriend, Christopher, proposed to her in Tuscany. Finally, she would get to have the wedding she had been planning since childhood.

Jenna came to us brimming with ideas. She was spirited and wise beyond her years, and she wanted a timeless, elegant wedding. Her optimism, her wit, and also her long brown hair called to mind another selfless princess bride: Belle, from Disney's *Beauty and the Beast*. In order to give Jenna a wedding that was worthy of her dreams, we would have to find a venue as stately and regal as Beast's castle.

We found our storybook setting at the Mar-a-Lago Club in Palm Beach, Florida. When Jenna first saw the gilded, Renaissance-inspired ballroom, laden with grand crystal chandeliers, she knew that it was the perfect place for her wedding. After the venue was chosen, Jenna and Christopher told us about their ideal reception.

She envisioned a formal, black-tie affair with music and dancing, and Christopher craved an elaborate dinner with fabulous food.

The Mar-a-Lago Club was the perfect location for Jenna and Christopher's wedding, because it provided the opportunity of staging all parts of the celebration—the ceremony, the cocktail hour, and the reception—in different environments. The couple chose the gilded ballroom for their traditional Jewish ceremony, a sunny pool area for an outdoor cocktail hour, and the club's grand ballroom for a reception with a four-course dinner and dancing. Once the details regarding the venue

were hammered out, it was time to send the invitations. Since Jenna wanted to convey the tone of a traditional, formal wedding, she chose cream-colored cards, to be printed with Victorian floral patterns in light pink.

With such a spectacular venue, it was important to design a wedding that would complement the beauty of the club—not mask it. Jenna had requested shades of pink for her décor, to which we added champagne gold, sage green, and traditional white. The first and most important task was to build the chuppah for the ceremony. In the Jewish faith, the chuppah represents the couple's new home together, so we wanted it to be comforting, intimate, and beautiful. With a structure of sculpted iron as the foundation, the chuppah was draped with sheer white fabric that came to a peak. Underneath the canopy, tea candles were hung with invisible thread, and a spherical floral arrangement that sparkled with crystals was suspended from the center. The front of the chuppah was decorated with hydrangeas, pink and white roses, and an abundance of sweet-scented white gardenias.

For a unique twist on the traditional white aisle runner, white petals were sprinkled down the middle of the walkway, and pink petals were sprinkled on either side. Several tall candleholders swathed in white fabric were placed along each side of the aisle in order to light the bride's path to her groom, and each was adorned with pink and white roses, in addition to dangling strands of rose petals.

When the guests arrived in their formal gowns and tuxedos, they were ushered toward several rows of Chiavari chairs that bordered each side of the aisle. A program that matched the wedding invitations sat on each chair, and Jenna's favorite Thoreau quote was printed inside: *There is no remedy for love but to love more.*

Since Jenna was such a loving person, she had often taken care of friends and family members without a thought for herself. Christopher wanted to give his bride the wedding of her dreams—a day that would be all about *her*—and he asked us to help him with a special surprise. Jenna was a violinist who loved classical music, so Christopher hired a string orchestra to play at their ceremony. As the groomsmen escorted the bridesmaids down the aisle, the orchestra played Vivaldi's *Four Seasons*—Jenna's favorite classical piece.

The three bridesmaids wore mauve silk gowns that were tied at the waist with burgundy satin sashes. They carried bouquets that matched the chuppah, each made of a different mixture of pink peonies, white roses, lilies of the valley, white cymbidium orchids, and brown galax leaves. Once they reached the chuppah, they turned and waited for the moment that everyone had been waiting for.

The doors of the ballroom opened, and

Jenna appeared in an elegant white satin gown. Crystals bordered the halter neckline, and satin bows trailed down the back of the gown to the end of the train. Her shoes were embellished with crystal accents that matched the design of her wedding ring, and her bridal bouquet was made of pink roses—the same flowers that Jenna's mother had carried on her wedding day. From the look on Jenna's face, it was clear to her friends and family that her childhood dreams of one day being a princess bride were coming true.

As Jenna started to walk down the aisle, a new song began to play. Only months before her wedding day, Jenna had lost her father, with whom she had had a very close relationship. Unable to have him escort her, she chose a poignant processional song as a tribute to him: "You Raise Me Up," by Josh Groban. All one hundred and fifty of her guests stood and watched, many with tears in their eyes, as Jenna met her mother and Christopher at the end of the aisle.

The cantor performed a Jewish ceremony that was personalized for Jenna and Christopher. The couple drank wine from the same kiddush cup that Jenna's mother and father had used on their wedding day, and recited their marriage vows. The ceremony ended with the traditional glass-breaking, eliciting cheers of *Mazel Tov!* from the guests. For the recessional, the orchestra played an

upbeat instrumental version of "All You Need Is Love" by the Beatles—perfectly fitting for the bride's outlook on life.

After the emotional ceremony, it was time to shift gears and set a tone of celebration for the reception party. We moved the guests outside, where a poolside cocktail hour awaited them. The repositioned string orchestra continued to serenade the guests as they mixed and mingled among white-gloved waiters

The Cocktail Hour

A COCKTAIL HOUR SERVES SEVERAL PURPOSES: it gives you a window of time in which to finish your wedding photography, it gives your guests a chance to stretch their legs before sitting down to dinner, and it encourages mingling among friends and family members who may not know one another well. Great food and beverages were

a priority for Jenna and Christopher, and their cocktail hour reflected that.

The general rule of thumb for passed hors d'oeuvres is to serve five hot dishes and five cold. Steer clear of skewers with dipping sauces—they can be awkward to serve and messy to eat. Choose a variety of foods with a variety of flavors, and make sure to include a few of your own favorites! Jenna and Christopher's hors d'oeuvres ranged from smoked mozzarella in profiterole to southwestern chicken with avocado salsa in blue-corn tortilla cups.

If you have the budget, food stations are a great addition to a cocktail hour. Some options to choose from are:

- Raw bars
- Sushi bars
- Stir-fry stations
- Pasta stations
- Culturally infused food stations, such as Spanish/Mexican, Pacific Rim, Hawaiian, Asian fusion, etc.

The stations at Jenna and Christopher's wedding served a broad spectrum of selections, from littleneck clams to smoked salmon to penne with wild mushrooms.

who carried silver trays of signature cocktails. Four different specialty drinks were offered, including fruit-infused Prosecco garnished with pear slices, and limoncello with lemon sorbet and mint.

Since Jenna and Christopher wanted to indulge their guests with delicious food, four buffet stations were set up around the perimeter of the pool. The couple had chosen each offering for a specific reason: a raw bar was meant to represent Christopher's family vacation house in Nantucket, where he and Jenna had taken their first trip together; a beef carving station (with a specialty sauce inspired by a recipe from Jenna's mother) was an homage to family holiday meals at Jenna's home; a sushi station alluded to a trip they took to Asia together with a group of friends; and a pasta station signified Christopher's proposal in Italy. Waiters passed around ten different kinds of hors d'oeuvres; each of which had been specifically selected by the bride and groom to be extensions of the four buffet themes.

The doors of the grand ballroom then opened to reveal a dinner reception beyond even Jenna's dreams. Huge arched windows, detailed crown moldings, and gorgeous crystal chandeliers made the room look as grand and royal as the ballroom in *Beauty and the Beast*. Two large, x-shaped table arrangements were set up in the center of the room, each composed of one square table and four double-length rectangular tables. Eight round tables were placed around the room to provide additional seating. This setup served a dual purpose: it occupied a large amount of space in a room that would otherwise have seemed too big for only 150 guests, and it allowed the guests to converse with people in multiple directions. It was no coincidence that the tables formed x's and o's. Those symbols, meaning "kisses and hugs," held special meaning for the bride and groom.

All the tables were covered in champagne-colored linen, and the x-shaped tables were topped with sheer table runners that were embroidered with flowers and leaves in green and gold. Low floral arrangements were placed at intervals down the centers of the long tables, and short white pillar candles contributed to the décor without preventing guests from seeing one another. Interspersed among the floral arrangements, antique silver candelabra held an abundance of tall white taper candles, giving the table design a formal, traditional feel. In the center of each x, a tall pedestal served as a base for a glorious floral

TUTERA TIP:

For your cocktail hour, request that your bars and stations be positioned far from the entryway. This will promote free and comfortable movement among your guests and prevents a bottleneck at the door.

When the cocktail hour was over, waiters led the guests back inside and into a marble foyer. There, guests encountered an escort card table topped with a huge urn that overflowed with flowers. The table itself was shaped like an x and draped in champagne-colored linen. Floral garlands flowed along the tables and down the sides, and, nestled among the blossoms, white candles gave the tables a romantic glow.

arrangement composed of green hydrangeas, white calla lilies, pink roses, three shades of pink orchids, and dangling strands of white and pink rose petals. The round tables were covered with sheer overlays that matched the embroidered table runners, and tall crystal candelabra in the center of each o held large floral arrangements that matched their x counterparts.

For their formal dinner, Jenna and Christopher wanted the presentation to be as mouthwatering as the food itself, so they chose dishes that encompassed a wide range of colors, styles, and flavors. Detailed garnishes and a variety of sauces gave the dishes a polished look that made guests feel as though they were dining in a five-star restaurant. The bridal couple also wanted their food to tell a

story. The dishes you select for your wedding reception reveal aspects of your personality, whether you choose a favorite pasta dish that your mother used to make, or a culture-infused dish that represents your heritage. The first course, sesame seared tuna in mango sauce, was an homage to Jenna's parents' wedding in Hawaii. The partygoers were then given the choice between two different entrées: Colorado rack of lamb, which was a tribute to Christopher's birthplace, and sea scallops, which represented Jenna's home state of Maine. The Belgian chocolate cake served for dessert was inspired by the European wedding of Christopher's parents.

WHEN SELECTING YOUR MENU, your goal is to be interesting and inventive, without overwhelming your guests' taste-buds with fancy foods that take them way out of their comfort zone. Remember: although your personal tastes are important, you are also catering—literally—to your guests' needs. At the same time, you should think of food selection as an art form, in which your canvas is the plate. Food is a part of your décor—a feast for your eyes and for your stomach—so it's important to experiment with different colors, textures, and flavor combinations. A perfect meal is comforting yet interesting, inviting yet chic.

When guests had had their fill of the delicious dinner, they made their way onto a large parquet dance floor that glowed softly with pink lights. A sixteen-piece band opened with "Endless Love," and Jenna and Christopher shared their first dance while their loved ones looked on. Then the party got into full swing, and the bridal couple and their fellow revelers danced the horah, a circle dance that is traditionally performed at Jewish weddings. The bride and groom and their parents were lifted up while

seated on chairs by their friends and family as the band played "Hava Nagila."

But the last course of Jenna and Christopher's delicious meal had yet to be served. Soon it was time for the cutting of their wedding cake, and the cake was everything a princess bride could hope for. Eight tiers of white cake were enveloped in white icing, and each tier was ornamented with a bow made of frosting that looked like the satin ribbons on the back of the bride's gown. Since Christopher

was such a foodie, we added a special surprise: each guest would receive a piece of the plain white cake, and then be invited to a toppings bar where they would be able to customize their cake with a plethora of tasty treats. Blueberries, strawberries, raspberries, melted dark chocolate, caramel sauce, and cherry sauce infused with Grand Marnier were just a few of the options. This not only delighted the guests—it involved them in the culinary experience. We encourage couples to make their cuisine unique and light-hearted—even in the most formal settings!

After the thoroughly indulgent dessert, guests resumed spinning about the dance floor to the melodies played by the energetic band. From the first notes of the processional to the final chord of the last dance, from the first sip of a cocktail to the last bite of wedding cake, the entire evening was an exquisite event that actualized Jenna's childhood dreams. At the end of the celebration, Jenna took a moment to throw her bouquet. In tossing those blossoms, she was passing her dream on to another girl, who would perhaps one day experience her own perfect wedding day.

OVERVIEW:

FASHION:

The bride wore an elegant white satin gown with a halter neckline that sparkled with crystals. Satin bows trailed down the back of her gown to the end of the train.

The bridesmaids wore mauve silk gowns that were tied at the waist with burgundy satin sashes.

INVITATION:

Cream-colored panel cards were printed with Victorian floral patterns in light pink.

COLOR SWATCHES/
FLORAL GUIDE

COLORS: white, cream, pink, green, gold

FLOWERS: white and pink roses, pink peonies, gardenias, white and green hydrangeas, white calla lilies, cherry blossom branches

SPECIALTY COCKTAIL:
LEMON DROP DREAM

4 oz. lemon sorbet (frozen), plus extra
for garnish

4 oz. champagne

1 oz. vodka

3 tb. whipping cream

Mint leaf for garnish

Spoon sorbet into blender. Add vodka and whipping
cream. Blend until smooth, about 1 minute. Pour
into a champagne glass and top with champagne.
Use a melon baller to scoop and add one or two
balls of lemon sorbet to the drink, and garnish with
mint leaf.

COCKTAIL MENU:

PASSED HORS D'OEUVRES

Crisp spinach and artichoke

Smoked mozzarella in profiterole

Beets in phyllo pastry

Miniature beef Wellington

Coconut langostino

Warm potato pancakes topped
with apple and pear chutney

Endive leaves filled with sweet-potato puree

Prosciutto, dates, and mascarpone
on walnut raisin crisps

Southwestern chicken with avocado salsa in
blue-corn tortilla cups

California rolls with wasabi, pickled ginger,
and soy dipping sauce

BUFFET STATIONS:

RAW BAR

Jumbo shrimp

Cherrystone and littleneck clams

Oysters

Crab Claws

Oyster crackers, lemon, sauce mignonette

STEAK HOUSE STATION

Grilled aged Black Angus sirloin

Creamed spinach

Homemade onion rings and potato chips

Three-peppercorn sauce
and horseradish cream

SMOKED FISH STATION

Smoked Scottish salmon, trout, and whitefish

Black bread tartines
and pumpernickel rounds

Capers, diced red onion, and lemon

PASTA STATION

Penne and orecchiette pasta

Wild mushrooms with truffle oil

Fresh tomato and basil with garlic

Shaved Parmesan cheese

DINNER MENU:

STARTERS

Sesame seared tuna with mango salsa

Seasonal vegetable soup

MAIN COURSE

Rack of lamb with tarragon jus, snap peas, Parmesan risotto, jicama, and phyllo crisp

Pan-seared sea scallops with wild mushrooms, truffle oil, mesclun greens, and asparagus

DESSERT

Warm Belgian chocolate cake with Grand Marnier–infused strawberries, Valrhona chocolate sauce, and vanilla bean ice cream

Wedding cake with toppings bar

MUSIC SUGGESTIONS:

FIRST DANCE

"Beauty and the Beast"
– Céline Dion and Peabo Bryson

"You and Me" – Lifehouse

FATHER-DAUGHTER DANCE

"No Matter What"
– from *Beauty and the Beast*
(the Broadway musical)

"You Light Up My Life" – LeAnn Rimes

MOTHER-SON DANCE

"Go the Distance" – Michael Bolton

"You're the Inspiration" – Chicago

DISNEY TOUCHES:
Beauty and the Beast

Nothing says "Be Our Guest" like delicious, well-presented food. Jenna and Christopher wanted food to be a primary focus of their wedding, so they made sure to indulge their guests with every course. For a *Beauty and the Beast*–inspired menu, choose French foods like cheese soufflé, quiche Lorraine, and chocolate mousse.

The flowers in a bride's bouquet say a lot about her personality. Family-oriented and traditional, Jenna wanted a wedding that would reflect those qualities. Her bouquet was made of pink roses—the same flowers that her mother carried on her wedding day. If you want to feel like Belle on your wedding day, you might consider a bouquet of crimson roses. After all, the story of *Beauty and the Beast* began with a single enchanted rose.

Nobody knows better than Lumiere how candlelight can create a romantic atmosphere. An abundance of silver candelabra and tall white taper candles gave a magical glow to Jenna and Christopher's reception. Choose golden candelabra instead, and you'll have a table setting fit for Beast's castle.

When designing the centerpieces for your dinner tables, it's important to remember that your guests should be able to see each other! For Jenna and Christopher's reception, we positioned lots of smaller floral arrangements down the center of each long table, allowing the partygoers to converse easily. If you'd like to invite Mrs. Potts and Cogsworth to attend your reception, rent several white teapots and small mantel clocks, and use them as bases for low floral arrangements.

For some couples, a ballroom with detailed ceilings, crystal chandeliers, and high arched windows is the perfect setting for a wedding. The ballroom at the Mar-a-Lago club certainly looked as if it could have been transplanted from a French palace. But if you like reading as much as Belle does, you might consider getting married at a library or a museum.

CHAPTER EIGHT

A Garden Dream Wedding

MANY STORIES ABOUT FAIRIES, elves, gnomes, and enchanted animals take place in gardens, and it's plain to see why. In a garden, the magic of nature is everywhere; it's in the flowers, the colors, the scents, and the wonder of life. It's no wonder that there is a feeling of mystery in places where beautiful things grow. In a garden, anything can happen.

It was that magical quality that led Charles and Michelette to choose a garden setting for their wedding. As soon as we met the happy couple, we discovered that their story was just as enchanting as any Disney fairy tale—it was just a bit more contemporary. Having both been married before, Michelette and Charles met on an Internet dating site. Charles was dashing and Michelette loved to sing opera. She also had a particularly large complement of aunts, so we couldn't help but think of her as a modern-day Princess Aurora.

The well-matched pair felt lucky that the paths of their lives had intersected, giving them a second chance at love. Well traveled, worldly, and wise, Charles and Michelette wanted to have a beautiful wedding that reflected the things in life that really mattered: family and love. Since they were both Italian, it was important that their celebration involve fantastic foods, wines, and a liberal dose of la dolce vita.

When they got engaged, Michelette and Charles had been together for ten years. He was already a part of her family, and she was a part of his. They had spent a decade together just enjoying their relationship, and the timing was finally right to solidify their commitment and celebrate it with their family and friends.

Wedding Timelines

TRADITIONAL STYLE: This is the most commonly occurring order of events, and it works well for many couples.

> **PRE-CEREMONY CELEBRATION:** guests mingle, sip champagne (thirty minutes)
>
> **CEREMONY:** (thirty minutes)
>
> **FORMAL COCKTAILS:** passed drinks and hors d'oeuvres (sixty minutes)
>
> **SEATED DINNER:** appetizer, second course, and main entrée. Each course is served, eaten, and cleared within thirty minutes. Important toasts and/or blessings and the first dance happen at the tail end of the meal (ninety minutes or less in total).
>
> **DESSERT AND DANCING:** the cake is cut and served. Desserts can also be served on buffet tables or passed by the waitstaff. A band or deejay performs and guests dance the night away.

COCKTAIL PARTY STYLE: This is a great way to change up the typical wedding timeline and to save money on catering. Note that it is very important to keep track of the pacing of a cocktail party sequence, so the celebration doesn't move along *too* quickly.

> **EVENING CEREMONY:** should begin about 8 p.m. (thirty minutes)
>
> **TRADITIONAL COCKTAIL HOUR:** passed drinks and hors d'oeuvres (sixty minutes)
>
> **BUFFET DINNER:** waiters bring out tables and a buffet is set with light fare (sixty minutes).
>
> **DESSERT:** sweets passed on trays with specialty after-dinner drinks (thirty minutes)
>
> **DANCING:** tables are cleared and a deejay plays until guests are ready to depart.

DINNER PARTY STYLE: This out-of-the-ordinary sequence is especially fun if you want to build camaraderie with all of your guests—before the ceremony!

> **COCKTAILS:** drinks and hors d' oeuvres passed as guests arrive (sixty minutes)
>
> **DINNER:** full sit-down meal with three courses (ninety minutes)
>
> **CEREMONY:** (thirty minutes)
>
> **RECEPTION:** the cake-cutting can be followed by toasts and the first dance. Additional desserts are passed or served buffet style while guests dance (ninety minutes).

Close friends had offered their home in Connecticut as a venue for the wedding, and Michelette was thrilled with the idea. With a lake on the property and a vast open lawn, we had plenty to work with in staging a charming cocktail hour, a distinctive tented dinner, and an unforgettable outdoor fall ceremony.

As with every wedding, the first step in setting the tone of the celebration is sending the Save-the-Date cards. For a simple, natural look, we chose white panel cards and letter-pressed them with only the very basic information: the couple's names, their wedding date, and the location. A few cream-colored branches and a tiny lavender butterfly accented the thinly scripted print, giving guests an insight into the elegant garden theme of Michelette and Charles's long-awaited nuptials. Later, invitations were created with the same white panel card material, which also featured the branch and butterfly design. Each invitation was tied with a piece of lavender raffia secured with a butterfly ornament.

The weeks leading up to the wedding flashed by, and soon, the big day had dawned. Guests arrived at the Connecticut estate at six o'clock in the evening, with the late summer sun still shining through the trees. A valet service tucked vehicles away into an unseen grassy area so as not to spoil the natural atmosphere, and the guests were ushered into a garden receiving area.

On a stone patio surrounded by butterfly bushes and roses, guests enjoyed lavender-infused martinis and rose-water cocktails. Waiters in long black ties passed hors d'oeuvres on hammered copper serving trays. The bride and groom greeted every guest, making sure to spend time with each person. A sense of togetherness permeated the garden as the two families—who already knew each other so well—regaled each other with stories of the bride and groom and prepared to celebrate their upcoming union.

TUTERA TIP:
Weddings require a lot of energy! In order to avoid becoming a sleeping beauty on your big day, make sure to get plenty of rest beforehand.

encountered two beautifully appointed dining tables that extended down the length of the entire tent. The tables were draped in sheer, almond-colored hand-woven linen featuring burgundy and gold velvet rosettes and hand-stitched green stems. In the center of each table, candelabras held white taper candles and served as the foundations for exquisite floral arrangements bursting with lavender roses, purple allium, green hydrangea, lavender calla lilies, pink anemones, pussy willow branches, pink dianthus, lavender, and green grapes. To make the guests feel like they were truly dining in a garden, we carried the floral element further by setting the tables with bouquets of lavender, white hydrangea, and pink allium in white ceramic containers painted with purple hearts. Wooden Chiavari chairs with gold cushions were placed around the tables, alluring guests to partake in the authentic Italian meal that awaited them.

Since Michelette and Charles wanted the food to be a focal point of their celebration, we

Following cocktails, guests were directed to a white tent erected on a grassy hill nearby. The tent was draped in white fabric, and the side panels had been gathered and tied back to create entranceways. Beautiful floral arrangements composed of pink anemones, winding green ivy, and pussy willow branches served as curtain ties. An escort card table outside the entrance of the tent held moss-covered boxes containing beds of lavender stalks. White cards in the shape of butterflies sat on top of the lavender, and each card had been letter pressed with a guest's name in delicate, light green script.

Once Michelette and Charles's guests entered the softly glowing tent, they

made sure to present it in a special way. Bowls and platters of different sizes and shapes held focaccia and Tuscan-style bread, marinated olives, Parmesan cheese, rosemary breadsticks, and sprigs of herbs. To further the garden theme with the place setting, we chose white charger plates with hand-painted green stems. For a bit of delicacy, white lace napkins were set on each charger plate and accented with a sprig of lavender secured with a faux butterfly.

Michelette and Charles did several things to make their dining experience a very intimate one. They dressed in evening wear that was on the casual side, and they sat in the middle of one of the long tables so that they could face their guests. When the food was served, it was done so family-style. The first course was a plated salad of Mediterranean vegetables, but after it was cleared, large bowls and platters of chicken, striped bass, roasted potatoes, and farfalle fra diavolo circulated among the guests.

Food Service Styles

BUFFET: For a buffet-style meal, food is set out on several large tables and guests are called up table by table to serve themselves. Buffets are a very convenient, but less formal style of food service for large events.

FAMILY STYLE: Each table of guests is served a large portion of each course, and then encouraged to pass the platters around—exactly like a family would eat dinner together at home. This is a good option for those looking for a service style that is a bit more formal than a buffet, but still casual and easy.

PLATED MEALS: With this more formal option, each individual plate is prepared in the kitchen and brought out ready to serve to each guest.

FRENCH SERVICE: Each course is plated at your table, prepared by table-side waiters who fill your plate from larger trays of food. This is considered very elegant, but it is also time-consuming.

RUSSIAN SERVICE: Food is pre-carved into serving sizes and then reassembled to appear whole. It is then brought out to your table and each serving is plated for each individual guest. This method is more formal than a family-style meal and takes less time than French service.

BALLET SERVICE: Ballet service is beautiful, but also quite expensive. One waiter serves each table simultaneously, and the waiters execute every motion in unison. It seems as though the waiters are performing the service, and it makes for a truly formal and special wedding meal.

While Michelette and Charles dined with their guests, they were entertained by strolling musicians; two accordion players and a pair of guitarists serenaded the party with Italian romance songs. Before the last course, the room quieted and Michelette and Charles exchanged bridal toasts. After sharing their insights on life and love, the couple joined in toasting their guests. The bride and groom thanked their friends and family for coming to their wedding, and for being an important part of their lives. When the toasts were finished, the sun had set.

While their guests were finishing their meals, Michelette and Charles got up from the dinner table and left quietly. After the last course had been cleared, the waiters announced to the guests that they would be departing for a new location. The well-sated partygoers joined their ushers on a walk that led right into the woods.

A candlelit pathway guided the revelers through the trees, while a small string orchestra played in a clearing nearby. The guests crossed a bridge where they found waiters who instructed them to line up on either side of a white fabric aisle runner that had been placed on the ground. Each guest then received a white candle to light

and hold. As if by magic, the music of *Cinema Paradiso*—Michelette and Charles's favorite Italian movie—wafted through the trees. Suddenly the bride and groom appeared in full wedding attire, Charles in a formal suit and Michelette in a beautiful white gown with an angelic veil covering her head.

Michelette carried a bridal bouquet created from sweet-smelling lavender, lavender roses, white lilac, muscari, and helleboris that were adorned with butterflies, ivy, and thin curving branches. The stems were wrapped in white satin accented with a sheer lavender ribbon, and a line of butterflies extended down the length of the handle.

Charles and Michelette walked silently down the aisle together, bordered on both sides by their friends and family. At the end of the aisle, Michelette and Charles turned around and asked the guests to follow them. As the light from their candles lit up the surroundings, the guests realized they were at the edge of a lake. A dock was floating by the shoreline, and a minister was waiting to perform the marriage ceremony.

The couple joined the minister on the dock, which was tethered to the shore with

TUTERA TIP:
If you are having an outdoor ceremony at night, make sure that the area is well lit. Unlike Prince Phillip, you won't have fairies to light your way!

two short ropes, and then the platform was released so that it could float partway out onto the water. Still close enough to the shore so that the guests could look on, the dock served as a stage for a very intimate service. A microphone amplified the couple's voices as they took their vows, and then a quartet from Michelette and Charles's church sang special arrangements of Beatles love songs.

When Charles kissed his new bride, all their guests applauded, hugged, and cried—as wedding guests are apt to do. Michelette and

Charles came ashore, and, with their family still holding candles, the happy couple recessed down the aisle to the jubilant melody of "Jesu, Joy of Man's Desiring." Then the bride and groom led their guests back through the woods to the tent where they would have a final, post-wedding celebration.

Michelette, Charles, and their guests re-entered the tent where they had earlier taken part in an Italian feast to find that it was now prepared for an elegant dessert party. Waiters passed silver trays of Italian dessert bites, including fruit tartlets with fresh raspberries, profiteroles, and tiramisu while the partygoers celebrated the marriage they had just witnessed.

Michelette and Charles may have planned many surprises for their guests, but there was one surprise that they did not know about. Michelette's sister had arranged to have an opera singer perform Schubert's "Ave Maria" at the end of the evening. Such a beautiful piece was well chosen for the overall tone of the evening, and it was fitting considering the bride's love of singing. The singer dedicated the performance to Michelette, and then shared a bit of history about the piece: "Ave Maria" was inspired by Sir Walter Scott's poem *The Lady of the Lake*, in which a woman prays to the Virgin Mary for safekeeping. It was a particularly moving story after Michelette's lake wedding, and a truly memorable gift from her sister.

After the performance, the couple and their guests danced to the lovely strains of the string orchestra. Finally, at the end of the night, a vintage car arrived to take Michelette and Charles to a Connecticut bed-and-breakfast. As the couple departed, their family and friends bid them luck and love, and thanked them for such a delightful, romantic evening.

Before the guests left the wedding, they were presented with favors that perpetuated the garden theme of the wedding. One gift was a small glass apothecary jar containing a bulb blooming with purple flowers and tied with lavender raffia and a butterfly ornament. The

other gift was a lacy white box of candies, tied in the same fashion. Michelette and Charles's guests went home with the knowledge that they had celebrated a relationship that would continue to bloom and grow.

OVERVIEW:

INVITATION:

Michelette and Charles's invitations were printed on white card stock and featured the same cream-colored branches and purple butterflies that had been introduced on the Save the Date cards. Each invitation was accented with lavender raffia and a butterfly ornament.

COLOR SWATCHES/
FLORAL GUIDE:

COLORS: lavender, pink, blue, green, cream, white

FLOWERS: lavender, allium, green hydrangea, lavender calla lilies, pink anemones, pussy willow branches, helleboris, white lilac, grape hyacinth, lavender roses, and pink dianthus

SPECIALTY DRINK:
LAVENDER GARDEN

1 ½ oz. vodka

½ oz. fresh lemon juice

¼ oz. lavender syrup

Frozen green grape for garnish

Fill a cocktail shaker with ice. Add the vodka, lemon juice, and lavender syrup and shake well. Strain into a chilled martini glass and garnish with the frozen green grape.

Menu:

PASSED HORS D'OEUVRES

Beet, maple, goat cheese, and walnut croquant

Daikon flower with smoked salmon butter and crispy capers

Toasted bruschetta with seasoned tomatoes

Speck ham canape with creamy apple and celery root

Crispy panko crab cakes with smoked jalapeño mayonnaise

Chicken and roasted pepper quesadillas with chipotle salsa

Sliced beef tenderloin with garlic mayonnaise and fresh Parmesan

ON THE TABLES

Rosemary breadsticks

Focaccia

Crusty Tuscan-style bread

Marinated olives

Parmesan cheese

FIRST COURSE

Mediterranean salad with artichokes, olives, peppers, and pesto dressing

FAMILY-STYLE DINNER

Chicken breast with pesto butter and tomato confit

Carolina striped bass with port wine jus

Roasted potatoes with rosemary

Farfalle fra diavolo with spicy shrimp

Asparagus with white truffle oil

DESSERT

Passion fruit tartlets with fresh raspberries

Key lime profiteroles dipped in white chocolate

Chocolate cups filled with tiramisu

Fresh fruit kabobs

Almond biscotti, cuccidata, and pignoli cookies

Pecan diamonds

Chocolate-covered cannoli

Music Suggestions:

FIRST DANCE

"Once Upon a Dream"
– from *Sleeping Beauty*

"Ave Maria" – Schubert

FATHER-DAUGHTER DANCE

"Thank You for Loving Me"
– Bon Jovi

"Dance with My Father"
 – Luther Vandross

MOTHER-SON DANCE

"The Rose" – Bette Midler

"You Are the Sunshine of My Life"
– Stevie Wonder

Favor:

Boxes of candy in lace packaging were tied with lavender raffia and a butterfly charm. Small glass apothecary jars containing flowering bulbs were decorated in the same way.

DISNEY TOUCHES:
Sleeping Beauty

✻ Your first dance can be as rehearsed or as casual as you want it to be, but make sure that you choose a song that fits your dancing style. A small string orchestra played at Michelette and Charles's reception, setting a classy tone for the celebration. You may choose a waltz like "Once Upon a Dream" from *Sleeping Beauty*, but you'll probably want to sign up for a dance lesson so that you and your groom can waltz as well as Princess Aurora and Prince Phillip.

✻ The shape and layout of your dinner tables can greatly influence the mood of your reception. Michelette and Charles chose to have two long tables and they elected to sit at the middle of their table as opposed to at the head. If you want to feel like you are feasting in King Stefan's castle, a long table might be a wonderful choice for your wedding.

✻ Having musicians perform during your reception can add a regal touch to the celebration. After all, King Stefan and his queen had a strolling minstrel who serenaded them during their meals. Michelette and Charles had three types of entertainers at their wedding: strolling guitarists and accordion players, a string orchestra, and an opera singer.

✻ The setting of a wedding is a primary focus for some couples, and a minor detail for others. Michelette and Andre's wedding took place in rural Connecticut and the natural setting played a large role in their nuptials. If you and your groom are outdoorsy, you may want to hold your wedding in a meadow, by a lake, or on a wooded cliff-top—perhaps like the one where Briar Rose met Phillip. However, if royal treatment is more your style, you could research renting a castle or a grand estate.

✻ Draping fabric throughout your reception space can transform it into a faraway land. For a *Sleeping Beauty*-inspired banquet hall, accent your space with swags of rich fabrics like brocade and velvet. Choose bold colors like crimson and purple, the color of royalty. You may even want to hang tapestries on the walls. Just make sure to leave out the spinning wheels!

CHAPTER NINE

A Modern Dream Wedding

MELISSA AND JOSHUA were the couple that every other couple wanted to be: they could glide across a dance floor as if they were the only two people in the world, and yet everyone else in the room couldn't tear their eyes away. This was only fitting, considering that these lovebirds literally met on a dance floor!

Melissa, an independent business consultant, was the kind of person who could multitask without anyone knowing, and she was always three steps ahead of the game, even when there was no work left to be done. Joshua was a diehard romantic who reminded Melissa to stop and smell the roses. These two were some duet. They needed a party that was exploding with fun, romance, and surprise, but also streamlined and cutting-edge—in other words, a combination of Melissa and Joshua.

The bride- and groom-to-be were full of great stories that gave us plenty of material to work with in conceiving both the overall design and the minute details of their wedding. This enabled us to personalize their celebration so that it told the story of Melissa and Joshua's relationship.

The couple's fateful first dance took place at a San Francisco nightclub. Joshua was living in San Francisco and working as an urban planner, and Melissa was on a business trip in the hilly city. After a long day of meetings, Melissa decided to drop in to a dance hall, and she met Joshua under the swirling lights of the disco ball. After she left town, John sent her postcards with different trolley cars on them until she finally came back.

Guest Transportation

It is customary to provide transportation for your guests if your venue is out of the way, or difficult to find (for example, up a mountain), or if parking is limited. Have your guests picked up at a prearranged meeting point, and have enough transportation to keep guests from waiting in line for a ride. It is also customary to provide special transportation for your bridal party, as they will be as dressed up as you will be, and it is in your best interest to keep them all together, to ensure that there are no stragglers! Keep the bridal party's transportation separate from the general guest transportation.

Although we used trolleys to move Melissa and Joshua's guests from the valet area to the party on this occasion, there are many other fun, unique ideas for wedding transportation that may work for you:

HORSE AND CARRIAGE	LIMOS
SPECIALLY DECORATED VANS	ANTIQUE CARS
LUXURY BUSES	EXOTIC SPORTS CARS
GOLF CARTS	MOPEDS
CUSTOMIZED CAR FLEET	RICKSHAWS
BOAT (IN APPROPRIATE LOCATIONS)	BICYCLES
	HOT AIR BALLOON
HAYRIDES	MOTORCYCLES

If you are providing transportation for your guests and/or your bridal party, your options may be limited by the size of your wedding and the capacity of the vehicles. Consider the following:

MODE OF TRANSPORT	PASSENGER CAPACITY
Van	6 to 12
Bus	25 to 50
Town Car	2 to 4
Limousine	6 to 12
Stretch Limo (SUV, Hummer)	12 to 30
Specialty Car (e.g., a vintage 1955 Rolls-Royce)	2 to 4
Sports Car	2

If you have buses bringing guests home from the venue, make sure that they depart in staggered runs. You don't want your guests to feel as though they're stuck at your venue! This may mean having smaller vehicles make several trips rather than asking everyone to wait to fill a fifty-passenger bus. If providing transportation for your bridal party is necessary, compare prices for limos, minivans, and party buses. Look for vintage cars or sports cars to rent. Alternative forms of transportation will give your wedding a fun, non-traditional spin—rickshaws, trolleys, and mopeds can provide great photo opportunities, too!

Also make sure to prepare a friend or family-member so that they can serve as the point of contact for guests who have questions (and they will). Alternatively, put all transportation information into an itinerary. You'll want to be able to do your own thing, come and go as you please, and not have to play chaperone the whole time. The point person should be the last to leave for the venue, and the last to depart the party, making sure everyone is taken care of. Choose someone outside of your bridal party—not a maid of honor who has to be somewhere at a certain time and could potentially leave guests hanging.

If you're serving alcohol at your wedding, have taxi companies at the ready. Call companies ahead of time and express interest in referring your guests to them, or hire a few town cars to run back and forth from your reception to your guests' hotels during the last hour of your reception.

If you are providing valet service at your wedding, remember that it is the first thing guests will experience—and also the last. Make sure the valet experience is smooth, calm, and organized during both arrivals and departures. Letting guests wait for their cars is not a good way to end the night! Before your wedding, make sure to choose a reputable company, and be in frequent communication with your head valet. Designate a point of contact to keep an eye on the valets and make sure that things are running smoothly. When using a valet service, one way to add a special touch is to leave a red rose with a thank-you note from the bride and groom in every car for guests to find at the end of the night.

Valet service is not a high-budget item; it just *feels* like one, and perhaps the very best thing about hiring a valet service to handle the parking at your wedding is the way it sets a graceful and well-orchestrated pace for the entire evening. At Melissa and Joshua's wedding, using valets served the dual purpose of preventing a traffic pile-up in the driveway, and giving guests the feeling of being transported into a parallel universe made just for the bride and groom. But the bottom line is pretty simple: even if you choose a simpler form of transportation, without as much personal significance, a valet shuttle can generate a sense of transition for your guests that feels invigorating and luxurious at once.

CONSIDER VALET SERVICE IF . . .

. . . you are inviting more than fifty guests.

. . . you are hosting your wedding at your home (or a private home) and parking is limited.

. . . you are opposed to people parking on your lawn.

. . . you are looking for a special way to set the tone of your event.

This story inspired us to add a unique element to their wedding: as guests arrived at Melissa's parents' house, they were directed by hostesses to leave their cars with a valet service and then board four shiny trolley cars that would take them to the ceremony location—a gorgeous white tent located atop a hill. The trolley drivers later reported that tales of Joshua's postcards circulated among almost every group of passengers during their rides to the ceremony.

Any aspect of a party, from design elements to escort cards to favors and even transportation, can be used as an instrument to provide more insight into a bride and groom's relationship. The trolley cars were a perfect way to share the couple's sweet story, add some delight and surprise for the guests, and turn what could have been an unremarkable transportation experience into an enjoyable and memorable moment.

We wanted to design a wedding ceremony for Melissa and Joshua that would achieve two main goals. First, to set the mood for what was sure to be a lively dance party of an evening while keeping with the elegant, modern concept of their celebration. Second—and most important—to create an atmosphere in which Melissa, the queen of multi-tasking and business deals, could mentally escape and live in the moment with Joshua.

The couple was certain that their ceremony should be held at the home of Melissa's parents. Her family had lots of property, which lent itself to the creation a magical world—and was also perfect for a tent. We decided to create a fantasy land, all in white, where the bride and groom would feel as if they were light years away from the hustle and bustle of the real world. To start, we draped the walls and ceiling of the tent in flowing white fabric. This simple act made a tremendous difference in the overall look, but we wanted the space to be more than just a tent; it needed to be intimate, elegant, and nothing short of jaw-dropping.

Six dramatic triangular archways were constructed with iron poles covered with drapery. These became the focal points for the room, and would also serve as the center aisle for the ceremony. Individual crystal chandeliers were suspended from each of the six archways. Along the sides of the aisle, custom-made Lucite containers were filled to brimming with rose petals, and pillar-shaped white candles were set on hidden stands inside each container, creating the illusion that the candles were floating on rose petals.

To really make the inside of the tent feel like another place and time, we chose to line the ground with a brown carpet, which set off the white fabric and ethereal arches. Melissa and Joshua chose to have a white aisle

runner that featured a hand-painted design depicting dozens of calla lilies with swirling brown arabesques.

The couple's chuppah needed to be the epitome of elegance. A single chandelier was suspended from the center of the pleated white canopy. Each of the four posts featured additional chandeliers with translucent white lamp shades on each candle, and each chandelier dripped with strands of long crystal roping, accented with white rose garlands. The back corners of the chuppah were adorned with three crystal chandeliers apiece, and two larger crystal chandeliers hung on either side. The resulting effect was ethereal, innovative, and idyllic.

The bridesmaids wore brown satin floor-length gowns, each with a thin silver ribbon around the bust. Long ribbons cascaded down the front of each gown. Melissa wanted each of her bridesmaids to feel as if she had a special role in the wedding, and we helped the bride achieve this by personalizing the bridesmaids' floral bouquets. We met with each bridesmaid and designed each bouquet to match her personality—a very easy adaptation to make to any wedding. Each bouquet differed in both style and the types of flowers used. Ranging from an upright gathering of calla lilies with a strand of orchids sweetly trailing down for Melissa's younger sister to a bold gathering of orchids and Casablanca lilies studded with diamond crystals for her gregarious best friend from college, the bouquets for Melissa's

Melissa carried a gorgeous, very modern bouquet of white orchids and white calla lilies, all of varying lengths. Around the stems, we wrapped strands of miniature pearls, to add personality to this very abstract arrangement that had been inspired by the calla-lily design on her aisle runner. After floating down the aisle to the delicate melody of Bach's *Air on the G String*, she met Joshua at the chuppah, where they exchanged their vows.

For the couple's reception, we sought to design an environment that was modern, elegant, and luxurious—as much swinging nightclub as opulent parlor. So, when Joshua and Melissa told us that they had lots of property and wanted to make the dance floor a highlight of their wedding space, we knew tenting was for them—double tenting, for that matter. The guests would move from the all-white ceremony tent to another, larger main tent for the reception.

bridesmaids allowed their individual traits to shine through.

Once the stage had been set, it was time for Melissa and Joshua to proclaim their love in front of all of their guests. The bride came down the aisle in a pristine white strapless gown with sparkling crystals all over the bodice. She looked as if she were made for her perfectly white surroundings, and it was difficult to tell whether her dress had been made to suit the venue or the other way around. Melissa's veil, trimmed in delicate white floral embroidery, added a soft touch that fit with the décor but also made the bride's beauty stand out amid the beauty of the ceremony.

The Tented Wedding

WHEREVER YOU STAGE YOUR CEREMONY and party, whether your guests need to feel as if they are in Morocco or eighteenth-century France, the principles outlined below can help you construct the perfect tent for your wedding. However, keep in mind that tents aren't for everyone. Permits need to be obtained, site inspections made, contracts signed, vendors hired. You are basically handing over control of your property to various companies for days, sometimes weeks, in advance of the wedding. Plus, for this wedding, we needed to install an air-conditioning system, complicated lighting rigs (i.e., stage lighting for the band), and a large quantity of rented furniture. So, although we absolutely love working with tents whenever we can—and they don't have to be quite as elaborate as the ones for Melissa and Joshua's bash— we would advise you to think carefully about all of the variables first. Here are the basic tenting options:

CENTURY TENTS: These are nice and tall and are structured around central poles usually about twenty-five feet high. They look like classic circus tents.

CLEAR TENTS: As with Julie and John's wedding in chapter one, a clear tent can be the perfect choice when you wed in a beautiful environment.

POLE TENTS: These have center poles and quarter poles down the sides. Pole tents have more exposed poles than do some other tents, but they are the easiest tents to install and the least expensive.

STRUCTURE TENT: A structure tent is installed with a steel support structure, parts of which will need to be camouflaged with fabric or other décor. It is our favorite type of tent, as it provides ample space. Structure tents are often used for concerts or large galas.

CHECKLIST FOR TENTED WEDDING

❏ **CAN WE GET PERMITS FOR TENT INSTALLATION?** Check local regulations. Though we installed the tents on Melissa's family's property, we still obtained permits from the city. As the four-week-long installation took place, the city made on-site inspections to determine whether or not all structures were up to code.

❏ **WHAT'S THE SOUND ORDINANCE IN THE AREA?** There are specific times during which music needs to shut down in certain towns. This is an especially important issue to consider if you are hoping for a wild, late-night party, or even just nighttime dancing.

❏ **IS THERE SPACE FOR THE CATERERS TO COOK AND PREPARE FOOD?** There needs to be ample room for the rentals, warming ovens, warming trays, and catering staff. Sometimes garages provide enough space, but extra tents are often required.

❏ **WILL YOUR BAND NEED A DRESSING ROOM?** Trailers were necessary for Melissa and Joshua's wedding band. Of course, some bands are happy to primp in a garage or a garden shed. Remember to check with your musicians beforehand.

❏ **WILL BUDGET PERMIT?** Tented parties are often the most expensive wedding venues. If your lawn is uneven you will have to have a level sub-floor built, which does add to the cost. (Avoiding a soggy or sloping dance floor is definitely worth the extra money.) You can talk to a tent rental company about what options you have to keep costs down. Bear in mind, however,

TUTERA TIP: *Consider your cooling options wisely if it's the summertime, and conversely, heat it up on cold nights: you can do a tented wedding in the dead of winter if you bring in a good heating system; in fact, it's easier to warm a tented space than it is to cool one. But in either case, there are several ways to handle temperature control. You can get an air-conditioning system, a heating system, or a system that can handle both. Temperature control requires power generators, which can be unsightly, expensive, and noisy. That's why we always recommend a "whisper system" generator—they are much less noisy. Unfortunately, they are still unsightly, so make sure that whoever installs them places them somewhere out of sight, earshot, and mind. A less expensive option is to add fans around the space— both standing fans and ceiling fans can be installed by the lighting company.*

that since you're creating the space from scratch, unexpected expenses will come into play. Be prepared for expenses relating to the tent itself, the flooring, carpet, dance floor, stage, kitchen tent, bathrooms, and temperature control.

❏ **WHERE ARE THE BATHROOMS?** For a party with over 100 guests, we insist on bathroom trailers. If you need to bring in extra bathroom facilities, always rent trailers, and create passageways between the trailers and the main tent with marquee tents. With porta-johns, don't forget to include the bathrooms in your overall décor. It's amazing how a few extra swatches of fabric can soften their look. We always leave a fragrant flower arrangement in the bathroom—gardenias, tuberose, lilies, and freesia are all wonderful choices. Scented candles, nice hand soaps, towels, and small baskets holding hand lotion, air spray, and breath mints can also make the most indecorous spaces feel civilized.

❏ **ARE THERE ANY STATE REGULATIONS ABOUT OPEN FLAMES FOR CANDLES, OR SIGNAGE FOR EMERGENCY EXITS?** This varies with location, but you need to check. Candlelight is part of many weddings, and parties can actually be shut down for lack of a properly placed exit sign!

A tent is a great solution for big weddings, which can feel cramped in ordinary indoor spaces and impersonal in huge ones. Tents give you full control over every single detail—the colors, layout, positioning, floors, and shape of the space.

For Melissa and Joshua's reception, we used a structure tent. It featured side panels that were thirteen feet high—as opposed to the standard eight—and a ceiling that was thirty-six feet high—rather than the standard twenty-two. Within the large main tent, we created a sense of movement by constructing a multi-level floor out of portable flooring material. The space included two intermediate areas that served as foyers leading into and out of the main space, two extended tented rooms for the caterers,

two raised dining areas, a two-tiered stage for the band, and a dramatic sunken dance floor. This mixture of elevations and passageways encouraged the guests to get up and move, and brought a sense of rhythm to the party.

Once the tent was constructed, our primary task was to fill the space with the right elements. Having too much furniture can cause the space to feel cluttered, and too little can make it feel awkwardly barren. Generating a sense of energy and motion in the party space is a key part of the process. Of course, this sense of energy was especially important for Melissa and Joshua's wedding. As Melissa put it at our very first meeting, "I want to see at least a hundred people—including my grandmother—still

Rental Companies

WHETHER YOU'RE GETTING MARRIED IN A HOTEL BALLROOM OR AT A RECEPTION HALL, in your home backyard or in a tent like Melissa and Joshua, rentals may come into play when preparing a space for your guests. If you're holding your event at a hotel or a venue that has wedding supplies, you shouldn't need to rent much at all. However, if you are planning a tented wedding, you will need to rent virtually everything. This can be really fun or somewhat daunting, so make sure that if you are planning a tented wedding, you're up for the rental challenge!

Every rental company has different products, so preview their goods online before you get to the showroom if you can. You'd be amazed at some of the things you can rent—whatever you need to build and set a table, a bar, or a buffet, right down to the linens and saltshakers. So if you're planning the wedding yourself, give serious thought to what you need in advance and try to stay focused. Rentals are also a great way to express your style and to further the theme of your party. Colors, styles, and textures of all things from charger plates to beautiful linen can transform your entire wedding into a picturesque dream. Here are some of the things you might consider renting:

CHAIRS

CUSHIONS

TABLES (COCKTAIL TABLES, DINNER TABLES, OTHER SMALL TABLES OR BARS)

CHINA (CHARGERS, DINNER PLATES, AND SALAD PLATES)

GLASSWARE

FLATWARE

SERVING PIECES

KITCHEN EQUIPMENT (CATERER USUALLY PROVIDES, BUT CHECK WITH CATERER FOR COST)

LINENS (TABLECLOTHS, NAPKINS, CHAIR COVERS OR BACKS)

COAT RACKS

FURNITURE

DANCE FLOORS*

*If your venue is outdoors, carpeted, or in need of visual uplift, you may want to bring in a dance floor. Some venues have these (hotels and reception halls, for certain) but for others that lack such resources, you may need to go through a party-rental company. Dance-floor styles can primarily be categorized as parquet (wooden pieces arranged in a pattern), black and white (alternating black-and-white squares like a checkerboard), all white, or customized (with a graphic, monogram, or special design that can be easily removed).

It's standard to allot about three square feet per person in determining how large your dance floor should be. You know best how dance-friendly your group of guests is, but we find that about thirty percent of the guests are on the dance floor at any given time.

working out their boogie fever at midnight!" Melissa and Joshua provided many of the cues necessary to make this happen, but a lot still depended on creating an exciting, energetic environment for the party.

Using Melissa and Joshua's tent and their yard as our blank slate, we built a fun, chic environment for their dance-themed wedding that we like to think of as disco moderne. Sleek, translucent "ghost" chairs and a color theme of white, chocolate brown, and ice blue definitely set a sophisticated, design-forward tone, but moderne never looked so groovy!

Modern design can give any wedding space a fresh, custom-made look, but in large doses its stark colors and bold shapes can also feel impersonal and even boring. That's why we always like to mix a variety of simple modern elements with something a little livelier. With the bulk of the surfaces in the space—from floor to ceiling—decked out in pure white, the striking accent colors blended with art deco floral patterns and a cool blue lighting scheme for a chic lounge feel.

Anyone who had ever spent time in Melissa and Joshua's living room knew about the couple's truly astonishing collection of vintage Lucite furniture, which was crowned with an eight-foot-long vintage dining room table made of solid Lucite. And every single one of their friends and family knew the significance of that table. Apparently, Melissa had fallen in love with the table at a New York antique store, but decided it wouldn't be practical to move it across the country. So Joshua tracked it down and surprised her with it when he asked her to move in with him. The rest is history, but it was also a key detail in the design scheme of the couple's wedding. Lucite cubes served as specially made shades for ornate chandeliers, creating a perfectly

personal tribute to the couple's love story.

We rounded out the rest of the party look with bold print fabrics, thousands of sparkling miniature disco balls to get the dancers started, and some fabulous customized banquettes—positively glistening in white vinyl. These touches ramped up the color and texture palettes of the party without taking away from the clean, tailor-made look. Last but not least, a generous mixture of roses, orchids, and calla lilies—Melissa's favorite flowers—gave the rigor of modern lines a sense of whimsy that was anything but minimal. The end result successfully combined the retro and the modern for a look that was unmistakably *right now*.

With the scene set to dance the night away in style, the next step was a given: selecting the perfect music to set the mood. Melissa and Joshua knew what song they would dance to even before they got engaged: KC and the Sunshine Band's "Keep It Comin' Love." This was the song that had gotten them both on the dance floor when they first met in San Francisco. As Melissa took a dance break, she looked around her reception and said, "I don't know what could have been more perfect. It's like our first night, but even better."

In the wee hours of the morning, the last guests finally boarded the trolley cars for one last ride. Upon receiving their cars back from the valet drivers, each guest discovered a special gift from the bridal couple: a tin of hot chocolate (straight from San Francisco) and, of course, a trolley-car postcard expressing the couple's thanks. It was a sweet ending to a truly magical night.

OVERVIEW:

FASHION:

The bride wore a strapless white satin gown with crystal embellishments.

The bridesmaids wore brown satin floor-length dresses with ribbon empire waists, V-necks, and thick straps.

INVITATION:

With sleek lines, shiny inks, and glossy textures, the wedding invitations had a decidedly contemporary feel. They were printed on glossy white stock with pewter-colored ink in a modern-looking font.

COLOR SWATCHES/
FLORAL GUIDE:

COLORS: white, silver, ice blue, chocolate brown, and cream

FLOWERS: white calla lilies, white orchids, white roses, Casablanca lilies, pale pink cymbidium orchids

SPECIALTY DRINK:
COOL BLUE MARTINI

2 oz. vodka

½ oz. blue curaçao

½ oz. white cranberry juice

Small white orchid bloom for garnish

Place all ingredients in cocktail shaker with ice and shake. Strain into chilled cocktail glass and garnish with floating orchid bloom.

Menu:

PASSED HORS D' OEUVRES

Foie gras on toasted brioche with ginger and rhubarb

Caprese skewer of tomato, mozzarella, and basil

Petite country ham biscuits with mascarpone and pepper jelly

Fried oysters on the half shell with pimento mayonnaise

Baby butter bean crostini

Kashmiri shrimp stick with ginger and coriander

Blackberry barbecued duck forks

Margarita-marinated soft shell crab in tortillas with arugula aioli

FIRST COURSE

Timbale of eastern blue crab, avocado, and roasted pepper topped with a Jonah crab claw, baby beet greens, and a roasted corn vinaigrette

ENTRÉE

Pan-roasted veal medallions with
sweet potato ravioli, veal-thyme jus,
exotic mushrooms, and buttered baby
Brussels sprouts

DESSERTS

Coconut marshmallow cubes

Raspberry tarts dusted
with powdered sugar

Mini chocolate volcanoes with edible
gold and chocolate fudge lava

Lemon meringue tarts

New York cheesecake with hot
caramel sauce

Petite pecan fudge squares

Triple layer chocolate brownie bites

LATE NIGHT NIBBLES

Mini cheeseburgers with pickle chips

Assorted mini pizzas

MUSIC SUGGESTIONS:

FIRST DANCE

"A Dream Is a Wish Your Heart Makes"
– from *Cinderella*

"My First, My Last, My Everything"
– Barry White

FATHER-DAUGHTER DANCE

"It Only Takes a Moment"
– Michael Crawford, from *WALL-E*

"Lullabye" – Billy Joel

MOTHER-SON DANCE

"Thank You" – Natalie Merchant

"In My Life" – the Beatles

FAVOR:

Tins of hot chocolate left in each car with a trolley-
car postcard thank-you note.

DISNEY TOUCHES:
— The Princess and the Frog

❋ Choose special transportation to get your guests where they're going—they will feel as if they're getting the royal treatment when they are whisked away to your wedding in a unique way, whether it's in a trolley car or a vintage car like Big Daddy LaBouff's in *The Princess and the Frog.*

❋ Music is an essential part of every wedding, and it often plays a key role in a couple's story. Melissa and Joshua's nuptials had a disco theme, but if you prefer jazz, like Prince Naveen, a live brass band is sure to get everyone's toes tappin'.

❋ Every couple has a story—even if it doesn't involve voodoo doctors or being transformed into frogs. Choose a few stories to share with your guests, and incorporate them into your wedding. Melissa and Joshua shared the story of their first meeting (on the dance floor), and their courtship (Joshua's trolley-car postcards).

❋ Let your party favors be reminiscent of your night. Melissa and Joshua's locally-made chocolate favors played into their San Francisco theme, but you might prefer to give out pralines—traditional candies from New Orleans made with sugar, butter, cream, and pecans.

❋ Choose a venue that has special significance. For Melissa and John we created a disco club on the bride's family's property. If you're more of a Dixieland gal like Princess Tiana, a Southern plantation, a French Quarter hotel, or a Mississippi riverboat might be the perfect setting for your celebration.

CHAPTER TEN

A Vintage Hollywood Dream Wedding

EVERYONE WHO HAS EVER been to Disneyland knows why it's the most magical place on earth. Where else can you visit Sleeping Beauty Castle, hug Mickey, and ride the Matterhorn? The land of Walt Disney's vision also exudes a sense of nostalgia for days gone by. Being on Main Street, U.S.A., in the Magic Kingdom takes us back to a time when *Steamboat Willie* was just being released, *Fantasia* was premiering in theaters, the first television sets were airing the ground-breaking *The Wonderful World of Disney*, and Orlando, Florida, was a distant dream. The 1940s were a time of ingenuity, glamour, and fashion—and there was no town more glamorous and fashionable than Hollywood.

When we first met Ashley and Jordan, they told us that they were in love with old Hollywood's sophistication and charm. They both had a great sense humor, an appreciation for the arts, and an original sense of style and flair. Jordan's trend-forward fashions were right off Rodeo Drive, and Ashley was never without a fascinating accessory: a consignment dress cut and converted into a fantastic waist sash, an antique locket, a pair of great vintage sunglasses with a matching head wrap, a small purse reconstructed out of her grandmother's antique lace doilies. And, of course, each accessory had its own story.

They were an affable couple, passionate about movies, having fun, and celebrating life. But the story of how they met was what really captivated our hearts. Ashley was an aspiring actress. She told us that one afternoon at a casting call, she fell and sprained her ankle while acting out a dance scene. Despite her injury, she got back on her feet and continued with the audition. But upon completing a difficult series of steps, a wave of dizziness hit her. Jordan, a film producer who was standing nearby, held Ashley's hand as he recounted the details of their meeting. He had noticed that she looked pale, rushed to her side, and helped her to a chaise lounge in the lobby. Ashley soon got her color back, but she never got her heart back; it had been swooped up by Jordan's gallant gesture. Their story reminded us so much of Snow White and her prince that we thought Disneyland would be the perfect place to hold their wedding. Since both Jordan and Ashley were big fans of Disney, they agreed wholeheartedly. Given their mutual love of fashion and film, we then decided that the concept for their wedding would be vintage Hollywood.

There was something magical about the era of old Hollywood, when black-and-white-film stars set the tone for glamorous living, and "style" was synonymous with the likes of Audrey Hepburn, Grace Kelly, Clark Gable, and Jimmy Stewart. The men were handsome and debonair and the women were graceful and elegant. Ashley and Jordan reminded us of a Tinseltown golden couple, and they wanted a wedding where every guest would feel the excitement and the passion of those silver screen glory days.

The couple chose to be married in Disneyland's Rose Garden, a quiet courtyard bordered by tall boxwood hedges and aromatic rose bushes. Its white gazebo would make a beautiful ceremony platform, and its impeccably manicured lawn was parted by a walkway that would serve as the aisle.

With the location finalized and the concept decided upon, we began to visualize how every detail of the wedding would play a role in contributing to the vintage Hollywood theme. From the invitation to the last dance of the night, every component would need to fit into the big picture while also drawing guests into the bride and groom's story. We began with the invitations—every couple's first opportunity to establish the style of their wedding. We wanted the invitations to set the Hollywood tone, convey the formality of the evening, and subtly introduce Ashley and Jordan's wedding style through colors and patterns. Most important, their invitation needed to make the statement that this wedding would

not be an ordinary celebration. As Cary Grant might say, it would be quite an affair to remember.

On each pale pink letter-pressed invitation, a black diamond-shaped pendant design was printed in the center, with the words, "An affair to remember." Small silver crystals added a hint of Hollywood glitz. The text inside the card combined black art deco lettering and bright pink script for an overall effect of understated elegance with a confident punch of color. A final touch of sparkle hinted that a special evening enchanted with Disney magic was in store for Ashley and Jordan's guests.

Our next goal was to craft a setting for the wedding that would create a time-transcending experience for the bride and groom and their guests. We began with the first scene that the guests would encounter: the Rose Garden's gazebo. Each pillar was wrapped with three tones of pink gossamer fabric (a light, medium, and bold pink), as were the banisters framing the steps. Along the sides of the gazebo, we hung curtains of white pearl strands accented with white gardenias.

A table was placed inside the gazebo and covered with sweet-smelling gardenias that would serve as a bed for the couple's unity candle. We also showered the gazebo steps

Fashion by Kirstie Kelly

To all the naysayers who swear that the days of old Hollywood glamour à la Audrey Hepburn and Grace Kelly have come and gone, the Disneyland Vintage Hollywood Wedding proves that glamour is alive and well. From heavy beading to intricate draping to the most seamless tailoring, no gown is too lavish for the ever-sensational vintage Hollywood themed wedding. Calling out to the boldest—and naturally, the most beautiful—brides and grooms of the world, a wedding of this caliber is all about being footloose and fancy free, and fashionable to boot.

A fit-and-flare gown that elegantly skimmed the bride's figure and showcased intricately embroidered lace took center stage in the vintage Hollywood wedding. Flattering on nearly any body type and size, fit-and-flare dresses were also a perfect shape for the bridesmaids, and echoed the bridal gown's silhouette making for a dramatic grouping. However, to avoid inadvertently stealing the bride's spotlight, the bridesmaid gowns were relatively unadorned.

Although the fit-and-flare gown could prove a match made in matrimonial heaven for any bride willing to occupy the spotlight, for the more conservative, a sheath or ball gown would be less body hugging, more forgiving, and thus a friendlier option.

Just as diamonds are a girl's best friends, accessories added pizzazz to this oh-so enchanting occasion. As seen here with Ashley, a tasteful shrug or shawl can tie a ravishing bridal look together and reveal a bride's personal sense of style. Pearl bracelets worn by the bridesmaids matched the bride's more elaborate pearl bracelet, and they served as bridesmaid gifts as well.

Besides the dramatic dress options and statement accessory pieces, daring color combinations enhanced the theatricality of the vintage Hollywood wedding; a black, white, and pink color scheme made for stark contrasts and instant glam. The black bridesmaid dresses were offset by the bride's white gown, and the flower girl wore a pink dress that rounded out the palette. The bridal party looked classic and modern at the same time, and the happy couple tied the knot with high style and bravura.

Hair and Makeup

WHEN SCHEDULING YOUR HAIR appointments for your wedding day, add a cushion of time so no one (neither you nor your bridesmaids) will be "fashionably late." Keep it simple! From ceremony to cake-cutting, weddings can be lengthy affairs, so your hair and makeup should be able to last all day. Start early on your wedding day and budget enough time so that you feel pampered—not rushed. Hire the right amount of makeup artists for your wedding party and remember, your wedding photos can't be retaken, so your bridesmaids need to look picture-perfect, too! Ask your makeup consultant in advance how much time she needs per girl, and how many assistants you need to hire in order to get the job done with time to spare for touch-ups.

TUTERA TIP:
Create a hair and makeup schedule for your bridal party. Put mothers of the bride and groom first, and the flower girl toward the end; kids love to play with their hair and face, so the shorter amount of time between your flower girl's styling and the wedding, the better. You, as the bride, are the final one to be done, saving the best for last.

with multi-toned pink rose petals. In order to create a dramatic look in the guest seating area, we color-blocked the ceremony chairs by alternating pairs of white and black Chiavari chairs covered with matching cushions.

Along the pathway to the gazebo, we placed black and white tufted vinyl stands that held floral arrangements in clear glass vases. The floral arrangements were bold, unusual, and very whimsical; each had several white calla lilies trained to curve at different angles stemming from a mass of feathers, white peonies, and black and silver ferns. White feathers trimmed the neck of each vase, and long strands of pearls dripping at different lengths drew parallels to the gazebo design. With all the arrangements facing inward toward the aisle, we had created an open-air archway for Ashley to walk through. The final touch was a beautifully bold aisle runner that was certain to turn heads. It was bright pink,

trimmed with black, and custom hand-painted with the couple's monogram and the pendant design that had been used on the invitations. The ceremony "stage" was set for our bride and groom, complete with an aisle more striking than a Hollywood red carpet.

Getting Ashley to assume the role of a Hollywood glamour queen was easy, but getting her to look the part would require careful attention to fashion, hair, and makeup.

In most cases, we say that less is more with regards to bridal makeup, but for this wedding, showy was the way to go. Ashley needed dramatic makeup and hair styling to match the time period, but she also needed it to be light enough to be comfortable for a springtime outdoor wedding. With inspiration drawn from Hollywood starlets like Marilyn Monroe, Bette Davis, and Judy Garland, Ashley's makeup was applied with two objectives: to accent her features and coloring, and also to match the style or theme of her wedding.

"*Something old, something new, something borrowed, something blue!*"

HERE ARE SOME SUGGESTIONS to help you adhere to the classic adage:

SOMETHING OLD: the string of pearls your mother wore on her wedding day; a bracelet that your grandfather gave to your grandmother; any family heirloom piece that has special meaning.

SOMETHING NEW: your new gown; the key to your new home sewn on the inside of your dress; a photo of you and your groom in a locket.

SOMETHING BORROWED: your mother's wedding band on your right hand; earrings borrowed from your sister; a purse from a grandmother.

SOMETHING BLUE: a bit of blue in your jewelry or hairpiece; a blue flower used in your bouquet; light blue embellishments on your garter; a pretty handkerchief.

Ashley's bridal bouquet was an extension of her starlet look. She carried a collection of pink calla lilies studded with pink Swarovski crystals and interspersed with white feathers. The handle of her bouquet was wrapped in white satin ribbon and secured with a strand of pearls around the top and bottom. A pearl brooch was fastened to the satin ribbon for an extra bit of flair.

Each bridesmaid bouquet made a different statement. One, made of bright pink roses and white feathers, had a light pink handle. Another bouquet of white peonies was bolstered with black and white zebra-striped feathers, and accented with pearls running up and down a white-ribbon handle. The last was designed with light pink roses studded with pearls and dramatized with black and silver ferns.

Before the ceremony, Ashley gave each bridesmaid a special token: a special silver sparkling brooch for the maid of honor, and faux diamond and pearl bracelets for each of the other bridesmaids. Ashley presented each gift in a box that was wrapped to evoke memories of Marilyn Monroe's famous "Diamonds Are a Girl's Best Friend" scene from *Gentlemen Prefer Blondes*, as she was giving diamonds to *her* best friends.

When the ceremony began, the brides-maids walked down the aisle, followed by Ashley's flower girl. She dropped pink rose petals out of an embroidered silk flower cone from the David Tutera for Disney Fairy Tale Weddings collection. Ashley and her father arrived at the edge of the Rose Garden in a vintage car. The fabulous pink aisle runner led the bride right into the arms of Jordan, her own debonair gentleman.

Once the bridal vows had been given, jazz-infused recessional music turned up the tempo of the celebration and lured the guests into a courtyard cocktail reception. The escort card table was draped in a black satin underlay and a sheer white overlay with tufted white florets. The name cards were displayed among bright pink rose blossoms, white gardenias, thousands of pink and white crystals, and long strands of white pearls. Three clear apothecary jars were clustered in one corner of the table: the first held black and white feathers, the second was filled with pink rose petals and oversized pink diamonds, and the last overflowed with pearls.

In the courtyard, a 1940s-style band played what Ashley and Jordan called "Swing and Sing" music—a myriad of classic standards ranging from Glenn Miller's "In the Mood" to the smooth sounds of Frank

Sinatra. White-tuxedoed waiters in matching white gloves pushed silver vintage bar carts, serving custom martinis and fine Napa Valley wines. Hors d'oeuvres were passed among the guests and included smoked salmon pinwheel lollipops and grilled shrimp cocktail martinis with lemon crème fraiche and crispy jalapeños.

Under the open California sky and towering palm trees, among the lush foliage of the Rose Garden courtyard, the guests enjoyed themselves as Ashley and Jordan posed for their wedding photos. In order to make sure that their memories were preserved, Ashley and Jordan had compiled a list of predetermined photos they wanted to take in their venue space. Disneyland's beautiful grounds and the Disneyland Hotel's waterfalls gave them plenty to work with! Thanks to this well-orchestrated plan, Ashley and Jordan were able to take their photos without any unnecessary maneuvering, and they still had some time left to join their guests for cocktails.

Photography

YOUR WEDDING DAY IS SOMETHING you'll want to remember forever, which is why it's so important for you to find the perfect photographer! It's essential that you like and feel very comfortable with your photographer, as you're going to be spending quite a bit of time having your pictures taken. In the months leading up to your wedding, meet with various photographers and get to know them; definitely don't rely on the quality of work in their portfolios or what you've seen online. Ask to see their work and discuss the styles you prefer. Schedule an engagement session, where you can test out your photographer's style, see their work (with you in it!), and begin to get comfortable posing with your fiancé in front of a flash.

Meet with your photographer to plan out when you should take your wedding photos—before, during, or after your ceremony. By taking all your photos before the ceremony, you get all of the shots on your wish list without losing valuable time during your cocktail hour. You also can take your time and have fun! While you forgo the tradition of "not seeing each other before the ceremony," overriding tradition may be worth being able to calmly get all the photos you need, and still have the time to spend with your guests on the day of the wedding. But that is a personal choice you need to make. If you decide to stick with tradition, just make sure you budget enough time into your post-ceremony schedule so you and your bridal party don't feel rushed!

Look into finishes and special effects, from sepia tones, to black-and-white printings, artistic colorings, and more. It's up to you to decide how much to manipulate your photos, but keep in mind that too much enhancement can take away from the realism of your wedding. Here are some options that you'll want to consider:

GLOSSY: A smooth, shiny coating on paper, like a mirrored surface. Glossy photos yield the richest colors and the sharpest contrasts.

LUSTER: A smooth surface that is less reflective than glossy, but still resists fingerprints. This is the finish used most commonly by professionals.

MATTE: A coated, no-shine finish. Colors appear softer, and while the photos are still high quality in terms of resolution, they have a duller tone.

WATERCOLOR: Photos are printed to look as if they were painted in watercolor. Sharpness and definition is replaced with gentle strokes and blurred lines, resulting in a more artistic (less photographic) rendition of your photos. These prints are often mounted on canvas.

Videography

FILM HAS THE POWER TO CAPTURE MEMORIES in a way that a still camera does not. Many couples choose to hire videographers so they can relive their memories in both sight and sound. You'll never want to forget the sight of your grandma dancing up a storm with your nieces and nephews, the sound of people's voices and laughter at your wedding, your first dance, and the facial expressions that went along with every special moment. Start selecting your videographer candidates based upon who has the best equipment. Don't hire a videographer that has lots of paraphernalia—in this case, less is more. Find a videographer who truly understands the meaning of capturing memories from your wedding on film; spontaneous moments can be the most precious!

Speak with your videographer about post-production special effects; slow motion, text, fades, and other videography editing tricks can be the defining line between classy and cheesy. If edits and special effects are done well, they can elevate the quality of the video to something far beyond what Uncle John could accomplish with his camcorder.

Ashley and Jordan made a fabulous videography favor for their guests. They had DVDs made with both a four-minute version and a twenty-minute version of the wedding and packaged them in black-and-white boxes along with their thank-you notes.

TUTERA TIP:
Make a video montage for your reception. Work with a videographer during the months before your wedding to compile a lovely five minute (or less) compilation of photos, video footage, and audio clips from both you and the groom.

Being so in love with film, Ashley and Jordan placed a heavy emphasis on having a videographer tape their entire evening. From the moment the couple began getting ready, through the ceremony, the bar-cart cocktail hour, and the dinner reception, Ashley and Jordan were filmed by a discreet videography team that captured every detail of the day. This would enable the couple to enjoy their wedding for years to come.

Working with their videographer in advance of the wedding date, Ashley and Jordan also used the cinematic element of their celebration to share their story with their guests. A large white projector screen adorned with pink and white flowers was set up in their cocktail-hour courtyard. As the end of the cocktail hour neared, a black-and-white video reel of Ashley and Jordan's relationship—backed by the score of Ashley's favorite classic movie, *Casablanca*—began to play. Vintage special effects (including deliberate cracks and discoloring) made the film feel like it was authentically old. The video montage not only furthered the style of their Hollywood wedding, it also created a smooth transition from the cocktail hour into the reception. As soon as the clip was over, the band played an

upbeat version of "Fly Me to the Moon," and guests were led into a nearby reception area of tables for "Act Two" of their evening in the Hollywood Hills.

Hollywood is larger than life, and we wanted Ashley and Jordan's reception to be a showstopper. The lawn adjoining the Disneyland Hotel was our canvas, and we let go of any décor inhibitions in true Hollywood fashion. Around the perimeter of the lawn we placed several giant, illuminated spheres that were suggestive of large pearls or bubbles of champagne. At the outset of the reception they glowed white, but as the night went on, they would change to pink.

In order to achieve the feel of a 1940s dinner club, we needed the table décor to be lavish and hip. Each circular table was first covered in a pink satin tablecloth, and then topped with black-and-white floral-printed linens with velvet appliqués. Since fashion was a huge inspiration for the party, we incorporated the couple's personal style into the table design as well. On the night that Ashley met her husband-to-be at the charity ball, she had worn a black gown with a butterfly cutaway that revealed a white sheath underneath. We translated this memory into the design of the chair-backs. Black Chiavari chairs with light pink cushions were covered with black fabric studded with pearl and diamond circular brooches. The brooches were pinned around the edge of a butterfly-shaped cutaway that revealed an underlay made of white feathers.

In the middle of each table, classic silver candelabras contained dramatic arrangements of white roses, black feathers, and pink tulips. Battery-operated taper candles set in the candelabras were covered with handmade, black-and-white-striped lampshades lined with pink braided trim and pearls. Strands of pearls adorned with gardenias cascaded down the arms of the candelabras, recalling the decoration of the ceremony gazebo. The base of each candelabra was covered in pearls, gardenias, and crystal flower-petal votives holding tea lights.

Coordinating with the silver candelabras, silver mirrored charger plates provided the base for each place setting. Silver ribbed flatware and squared clear glassware lent a progressive feeling to each table, and sheer pink napkins were folded into roses atop each charger plate. In order to complete the look, vertical menu cards were letter-pressed in pink, studded with tiny white pearls, and printed with the monogram-pendant design that was first used on the invitations.

In keeping with the theme of vintage Hollywood, the Disney chefs created a menu that put new twists on delicious classics. The first course was a deconstructed fruit cocktail with melon caviar, arranged in a colorful, checkerboard design. The second course was comprised of a small sunny-side up quail egg on toast, prosciutto, and a double-shot of orange juice. For the third course, each guest was presented with a pepper-crusted petite filet with a bourbon reduction, a baby baked potato, and mini onion rings. And lastly, dessert came in the form of heart-shaped, pink and black-frosted sugar cookies served with double-shots of milk. The meal was

everything Ashley and Jordan wanted it to be: unpredictable, lighthearted, youthful, and fun.

Throughout dinner a pianist played a white grand piano as a sultry lounge singer crooned the hits of Judy Garland, Doris Day, and the Andrews Sisters. After finishing the meal, Ashley and Jordan stepped over to a cake table, entirely covered in cascading white feathers. Set on a dramatic black stand, the four-tiered, square cake was covered in fondant and decorated with pink trim, black scrollwork, and sugar sculpted brooches and pendants in pinks, pearly whites, and silvers.

After the cake-cutting, the soft piano music was replaced by a lively jazz deejay. Guests danced on the lawn among the lit spheres until they retired to their rooms in the historic Disneyland Hotel. The following morning, the newlyweds hosted a rooftop send-off brunch at the Grand Californian Hotel, at which point they gave their guests the customized DVD favors that commemorated their one-of-a-kind celebration.

Ashley and Jordan had hosted a magical night that celebrated the kind of love they thought could only be found in the movies. All of the actors, props, costumes, and special effects had come together at the happiest place on earth to create a production that was glamorous, lavish, and sophisticated—everything that typified Hollywood's golden age. And the best part was that Ashley and Jordan's love story was just beginning; they had a lifetime to complete their movie together.

OVERVIEW:

FASHION:

The bride wore a strapless, form-fitting netted-lace wedding gown from the Disney Bridal Giselle collection. The empire bodice was ruched and the tulip-cut skirt flared into a sophisticated train.

The bridesmaids wore black Dupioni strapless dresses from the Snow White Maidens collection. The trumpet silhouette was enhanced with a pleated bust, ruffles along the bust line, and a short chapel train.

INVITATION:

Ashley and Jordan's vintage Hollywood invitations were printed in a Copperplate Gothic font in black ink on white card stock. They were accented with shades of pink, crystals, feathers, and pearls. The envelopes were black with pearl-colored lining.

COLOR SWATCHES/ FLORAL GUIDE:

COLORS: dark pink, light pink, white, black, silver

FLOWERS: pink tulips, white calla lilies, dark and light pink roses, white roses, gardenias, tree ferns

SPECIALTY DRINK:
THE ROSE GARDEN MARTINI

2 ½ oz. vodka

4 to 5 drops rose water

Simple syrup

Rose petals for garnish

Roughly chop a few rose petals. Dip half the rim of the martini glass into the simple syrup. Blot with a towel to prevent syrup from running down the glass. Dip the glass into the chopped rose petals. Add vodka, ice, and rose water to a martini shaker. Shake and strain into rose-petal-rimmed glass. Garnish with a single floating rose petal.

Menu:

HORS D'OEUVRES

Smoked salmon pinwheel lollipops

Grilled shrimp cocktail martinis with lemon crème fraiche and crispy jalapeños

FIRST COURSE

Deconstructed fruit cocktail with melon caviar and sweet balsamic dressing

SECOND COURSE

Sunny-side up quail egg on toast, prosciutto, and orange juice shot

THIRD COURSE

Pepper-crusted petite filet with bourbon reduction, baby baked potato, mini onion rings

DESSERT

Wedding cake

Heart-shaped pink and black-frosted sugar cookies with milk

Music Suggestions:

FIRST DANCE

"Someday My Prince Will Come" – from *Snow White and the Seven Dwarfs*

"Everything" – Michael Bublé

FATHER-DAUGHTER DANCE

"The Way You Look Tonight" – Frank Sinatra

"Just the Way You Are" – Billy Joel

MOTHER-SON DANCE

"My Wish" – Rascal Flatts

"Because You Loved Me" – Céline Dion

Favor:

Ashley and Jordan's videographer made custom DVDs of their wedding day, including both a four-minute version and a twenty-minute version, so that the couple could give these as favors at their send-off brunch the following morning.

Disney Touches:
Snow White and the Seven Dwarfs

If there is no room in your budget for expensive napkin rings, consider a beautiful and original napkin treatment. We folded pink napkins into roses for Ashley and Jordan's wedding, but for *Snow White*-inspired place-settings, you could accent white napkins with small dove charms that look like the doves who keep Snow White company while she scrubs the castle courtyard.

Your hairstyle is just as much a part of your look as your wedding gown. Snow White's classic coif is sleek, short, and simple—similar to the styles of 1940s starlets. Ashley wanted something similar for her hair, so she had it done in a chic chignon at the base of her neck.

Add intricate details to your décor to help tell your story. Ashley and Jordan had a stylish wedding with feather accents, brooches on chair-backs, and pearls on the candelabras and tables. Since the Seven Dwarfs are jewel miners, you might want to incorporate gemstones into your wedding decorations by filling mason jars with faux rubies and emeralds or affixing diamond and sapphire rhinestones to your menu cards.

Snow White's mother wished for a child with skin as white as snow and hair as black as ebony. For a glamorous wedding color scheme, use black and white as the main colors and choose a bold accent color like red or pink to create a striking, sophisticated look.

Choose desserts that play into your theme. Ashley and Jordan served both wedding cake and heart-shaped cookies that were decorated with their wedding colors. For a *Snow White*-inspired treat, ask your caterer to make candied apples or serve apple crumble along with your wedding cake. You might even be able to request an apple spice wedding cake with fresh fruit filling!

Vendor Directory

AIR DIMENSIONAL DESIGN
Ph: (818) 765-8100
www.airdd.com
Lighting
Vintage Hollywood wedding

ANTIQUE PURSES BY JILL
Ph: (248) 857-8822
www.antiquepursesbyjill.com
Antique purses
Country wedding

**THE BARNS AT WESLEYAN HILLS
PRESENTED BY PAVILION CATERING**
Ph: (860) 347-7171
www.pavilioncatering.com
Venue
Country wedding

BUDDAKAN
Ph: (212) 989-6699
www.buddakannyc.com
Venue and catering
Asian wedding

CAKES BY JAY
Ph: (516) 674-8115
www.jayscakecouture.com
Cakes
Sparkle and Country weddings

**CAKES BY THE "POUND" BY MENDY
K. POUND**
Ph: (626) 233-2748
www.cakesbythepound.com
Cakes
Vintage Hollywood wedding

CeCi NEW YORK
Ph: (212) 989-0695
www.cecinewyork.com
Invitations
Sparkle, Asian, Country, Garden,
Beach, and Indian weddings

**CLASSIC PARTY RENTALS EVENT
SPECIALISTS**
Ph: (212) 752-7661
www.classicpartyrentals.com
Event rentals
Vintage Hollywood, Beach, and
Indian weddings

CLOTH CONNECTION
Ph: (845) 426-3500
www.clothconnection.com
Linens
Disney Dream and Beach
weddings

CREATIVE GIFTS INTERNATIONAL
Ph: (800) 245-0427
www.creativegiftsdirect.com
Favors
Beach wedding

CUDGE.NET
www.cudge.net
Votives
Asian wedding

DC RENTAL
Ph: (703) 671-7300
www.dcrental.com
Event rentals
Country wedding

DELAWARE VALLEY FLORAL GROUP
Ph: (800) 676-1212
www.dvflora.com
Flowers
Country, Vintage Hollywood, and
Asian weddings

**DESIGNER 8* EVENT FURNITURE
RENTALS**
Ph: (323) 962-2062
www.designer8furniturerental.
com
Aisle stands
Vintage Hollywood wedding

EAST SIX
Ph: (212) 665-4846
www.eastsix.com
Invitations
Vintage Hollywood wedding

THE FEATHER PLACE
Ph: (212) 921-4452
www.thefeatherplace.com
Feathers
Vintage Hollywood wedding

HEARTFELT WISHES
Ph: (973) 383-6760
www.heartfeltwishes2u.com
Favors
Garden wedding

KATE ASPEN
Ph: (866) 446-1577
www.kateaspen.com
Favors
Country wedding

MAGNOLIAS LINENS, LLC
Ph: (212) 472-7708
www.magnoliasgroup.com
Linens
Country wedding

MARIA THOMAS OF PENDRAGON INK
Ph: (508) 234-6843
www.mariathomasonline.com
Printed materials
Disney Dream wedding

THE ORIGINAL RUNNER COMPANY
Ph: (212) 246-6600
www.originalrunners.com
Hand-painted aisle runners
Vintage Hollywood and Asian
weddings

PARK AVENUE CANDLES
Ph: (800) 328-3378
www.parkavenuecandles.com
Candles
Country wedding

PARTY CLOTH
Ph: (888) 232-7156
www.partyclothsnewyork.com
Linens
Indian, Modern, and Traditional
weddings

PARTY RENTAL LTD.
Ph: (201) 727-4700
www.partyrentalltd.com
Event rentals
Asian and Indian weddings

ROOST
Ph: (415) 339-9500
www.roostco.com
Furnishings and décor elements
Country wedding

SCRIBE INK CALLIGRAPHY
Ph: (212) 249-1817
Scribeinkcalligraphy.com
Calligraphy
Sparkle wedding

SONNIER & CASTLE
Ph: (212) 957-6481
www.sonnier-castle.com
Catering
Indian and Beach weddings

THE TOTAL TABLE
Ph: (610) 651-2724
www.TotalTable.com
Linens
Garden wedding

WILDFLOWER LINEN
Ph: (866) 965-7775
www.wildflowerlinens.com
Linens
Vintage Hollywood and Asian
weddings

WILDFLOWERS BY LORI
Ph: (856) 459-3515
www.wildflowersbylori.com
Cakes
Asian wedding

WILEY VALENTINE
Ph: (949) 764-9338
www.wileyvalentine.com
Invitations
Modern and Traditional weddings

Acknowledgments

I extend my heartfelt thanks:

To the vendors who have contributed their time and valuable resources to the making of this book, and to the incredible Disney's Fairy Tale Weddings team: Tim Hill, Korri McFann, and Cindy Garber.

To Ryan Jurica — Thank you for bringing a special kind of magic into my life and into my work. In all that you do, you are my greatest support, my best friend . . . and my happily ever after.

To Liz Hart — Thank you for your incredible writing and creativity and for making this wedding book truly one that is unique and special. Liz, you are my Tinker Bell, and I am convinced you spread pixie dust every day.

To my staff at David Tutera, Inc., with special mention to Jaclyn Steudtner, whose vision and resourcefulness spin straw into gold at every photo shoot, and to Christine Fontanazza, who brings life to my ideas and can do anything with her magic wand.

To the photographers, who masterfully captured images of the love these couples shared and of my love for design. A special thank you to my friends and colleagues, Jennifer and Charlie Maring. I also send my gratitude to the talented Michael Bennett Kress and Associates, Arden Ward, Phil Kramer Photography, and Gary Zindel Photographers.

And to my parents, Joe and Jo Ann Tutera — Thank you for teaching me the magic of love and family, and for introducing me to the wonders of Disney World from the very beginning. I love you.

David Tutera